BIG CHEVYS

A SOURCE BOOK

EDITED AND ANNOTATED BY

Edward A. Lehwald

Motorbooks International
Publishers & Wholesalers Inc.
Osceola, Wisconsin 54020, USA

Bookman Publishing/Baltimore, Maryland

Printed in the U.S.A.
Copyright 1983 in U.S.A. by Bookman Dan!, Inc.

ISBN 0-934780-25-0

First Edition
First Printing

Inquiries may be directed to:
Bookman Dan!, Inc.
P.O. Box 13492
Baltimore, Maryland 21203

Book trade distribution by:
Motorbooks International
P. O. Box 2
Osceola, Wisconsin 54020

Contents

Preface

The performance era of the big Chevys started with the "hot ones" of 1955-57. Although Chevrolet did not completely own the stock and drag tracks during the next 15 years, it certainly made its product known from local meets to NASCAR. This book details the story of the cars, engines and options available during this period by telling the story in the words of the manufacturer as published in its sales literature. Some of this material, such as the first Impala SS catalogue, is so rare that few enthusiasts have ever seen it. Indeed, some of the rarer pieces of this material can command prices of $100 or more from sales literature dealers.

This volume compliments my Chevelle SS and Nova SS volumes already published in Bookman Publishing's Source Book series. It differs from other volumes in that series in that it deals with all of the V-8 models rather than with just one series. This book originally started out to be an Impala SS Source Book but, on a few moments reflection, it became apparent that to limit the book to a discussion on the SS alone would not fully tell the performance story of the big Chevys since Chevrolét was loath to restrict engine and performance options to selected models as Chevelle and Nova did. Thus, you were as likely to see a Biscayne as an Impala on the stock tracks. I have, however, emphasized the V-8 engines and performance options in this book.

The Impala SS was, of course, among the most beautiful and exciting of the big Chevys but it never achieved, in its own right, the true performance status of, say, the Chevelle SS, Nova SS or Camaro SS. Whether this was due to fuzzy thinking on the part of Chevrolet brass or on marketplace realities is a matter of conjecture and debate which will probably never be resolved. Whatever the reason, "She's real fine, my 409" was a phrase said with pride by a generation of high school and college kids. The story of the 409 engine and its high-powered siblings is told here in detail.

While no other book has presented the big Chevy story, and much of this material, before there are several other books which provide interesting background on other aspects of the big Chevys story. These books have provided a partial reference for this book and are recommended to the interested reader. First and foremost, for the performance enthusiasts is Terry Boyce's excellent "Chevy Super Sports 1961-1976." For those interested in the 55-57 Chevys there is always Pat Chappel's "The Hot One: Chevrolet 1955-57." Although a bit dated now, George Dammann's "Sixty Years of Chevrolet" is still a valuable reference. The Chevrolet section of "The Encyclopedia of American Supercars" by Robert C. Ackerson contains important information of interest to enthusiasts of these cars. Finally, the Chevrolet section written by Tony Hossain for the Old Cars' "Standard Catalogue of American Cars 1946-1975" provides much valuable detail on specifications, technical changes and optionally available equipment although the format used by the book makes it a bit daunting to wade through to find what you want.

Production figure information is always challenging to find. The data quoted in this book was based first on information provided by Chevrolet. This, alas, is not always as complete as one would wish. Therefore, secondary sources have been used to supplement it. First, Jerry Heasley's "Production Figure Book for US Cars" was used, then "Sixty Years of Chevrolet," "Chevy Super Sports 1961-1976" (for Impala SS), the "Standard Catalogue of American Cars 1946-75," and, finally, Richard Langworth's "Encyclopedia of American Cars" (in that order). In the few cases where there was conflict or disagreement over specific production figures, the author's judgement was used to arbitrate. Weights and price datas were taken from the N.A.D.A. guides. Again, even this source is not always consistent from volume to volume on reported weight and price data. In the few cases where there were differences, the latest published edition to cover the car in question was used.

The intention of a book in the Source Book series (see page 144 for a current list of all Source Books in print as of publication date) is not to reproduce all of the available manufacturer's sales literature produced each year. That would be repetative and boring since frequently identical words and pictures were used in several publications. This book does reproduce all of the significant material produced with regard to the V-8 engines and the models associated with them.

Nor has it been possible to reproduce the sales literature in its original size. However, every effort has been made to make the material readable and useful. In each year the covers of the Chevrolet and GM full-line catalogues are reproduced so that collectors will have an easy time at flea markets identifying material for their collections.

Although great care has been taken to present complete coverage of each model as accurately as possible, it is possible that errors of omission or commission have occured. If any reader discovers such an error, I would like to hear of it (write to me in care of my publisher) so that it can be corrected in future editions.

No work of this size is ever a one-man effort. I would like to thank Tom Bonsall and Robert Tuthill for the sales literature supplied from their extensive collections. Tom is also my editor and no better editor can be found. Without the help of these gentlemen, this book would have been impossible. Needless to say, however, while they get to share in any credits which accrue, they are absolved of any blame for the book's weaknesses.

Baltimore, Maryland
October, 1983

This was the year that Chevrolet would reach out and grab the initiative in postwar automotive design. In so doing it also set a blistering pace with its splendid new OHV V-8 for its competition during the next 15 years of the musclecar power derby.

In 1955, Chevy continued to offer sixteen models in three series: the "One-Fifty," "Two-Ten," and Bel Air. Each of these was new this year from the frame up. This attractive design would later be recognized as one of the ten best automotive designs in history by Life Magazine's panel of automotive experts.

As stunning as the visual differences were between the 1954 and 1955 models, external dimensions were almost the same. The wheelbase remained 115" while overall length increased by a mere .6". Width decreased three-quarters of an inch to 74". (Station wagons were 197.1" in length.)

Without minimizing the new body and the mechanical improvements (like the new front suspension), the really big news this year was the introduction of the 265 cu. in. OHV V-8 which would turn out 160-hp at 4400 RPM with manual transmission or 170-hp at 4400 RPM with Powerglide transmission. Even in standard form this was sizzling performance by past Chevy standards. Equipped with the "power-pack" option which included dual exhausts and a single, four-barrel carb, this wonder-engine would turn out

180-hp at 4600 RPM. The brain child of Chevrolet's Ed Cole and Harry Barr, this engine was destined to achieve immortality as the father of the small-block 283, fuel-injected V-8. In its 265 cu. in. form, this engine (with the power-pack and 8:1 compression ratio) won its class championship at Daytona in the "flying mile" with a speed of 112.877 mph and in acceleration runs with 78.158 mph.

It is interesting to note that a four-door Bel Air equipped with the V-8 actually dropped 30 lbs. in weight over the equivalent 1954 model, although it added $99 in price. Model year production for the "One-Fifty" series was 134,257 and for the "Two-Ten" series, 805,309. Bel Air model year production totalled 773,238, of which 8,386 were the mid-year Nomad Station Wagon. A V-8 equipped Bel Air cost: $2,031 for the four-door sedan; $1,987 for the two-door sedan; $2,166 for the Sport Coupe; $2,305, convertible; $2,361, Beauville Station Wagon; and, $2,571 for the Nomad.

Literature for 1955 was plentiful. The full-line Chevy catalogue (pages 8-11 and 14) was supplemented with a station wagon piece (cover shown below) as well as an smaller "saver" folder (pages 12-13). There was also an interesting series of performance-oriented ads (pages 15-18).

Here It Is:
THE NEW CHEVROLET V8 ENGINE!

Here's the valve-in-head V8 as only the valve-in-head leader can build it. And here are some of the wonderful things it brings you: 162 horsepower with an 8-to-1 ultra-high compression ratio! Highly efficient oversquare design, which means less piston travel . . . less friction wear! Exceptionally high horsepower per pound! The great new Chevrolet V8 delivers brilliant performance, surprisingly high gas mileage, and extra long life.

Extra! The new Plus-Power Package boosts Chevrolet's V8 horsepower to 180 . . . brings you even more exciting performance! Optional at extra cost on V8 models.

NEW 12-VOLT ELECTRICAL SYSTEM

A new 12-volt electrical system provides greater generator capacity . . . finer high-speed performance . . . more efficient battery charging . . . quicker, easier cold-weather starting! You get this engineering advance with all three 1955 Chevrolet engines!

THE BIGGEST POWER-DRIVE CHOICE IN CHEVROLET HISTORY!

In the new Chevrolet you have your choice of three great valve-in-head engines, including the new V8—and your choice of three advanced drives, including the new Touch-Down Overdrive. All in all, you can select from six different power-drive combinations (as shown in the table at right)—the biggest choice in Chevrolet history! You get power as you like it in Chevrolet for '55!

TAKE YOUR CHOICE OF 6 NEW POWER TEAMS

1	2	3
123 h.p. SIX with Standard Transmission	123 h.p. SIX with OVERDRIVE	136 h.p. SIX with POWERGLIDE

4	5	6
162 h.p. V8 with Standard Transmission	162 h.p. V8 with OVERDRIVE	162 h.p. V8 with POWERGLIDE

Both Overdrive and Powerglide Power Teams optional at extra cost.

NEW TOUCH-DOWN OVERDRIVE

Here's great new driving flexibility and wonderfully responsive performance combined with big gas savings! Teamed with either the new 123-h.p. six or the great new V8 and new Power-Master rear axle, it's optional on all models at extra cost.

NEW HEAVY-DUTY SYNCHRO-MESH TRANSMISSION

The new heavy-duty synchro-mesh transmission offers the very finest in standard driving with outstanding gasoline economy. It brings you extra durability—plus extra-smooth operation. Teamed with Fuel-Saver axle and either the new 123-h.p. six or the great new V8.

IMPROVED, SUPER-SMOOTH POWERGLIDE

America's most popular automatic transmission is smoother, quieter and thriftier than ever for '55! New engineering advances keep Powerglide's automatic shifts from low to cruising range a smooth, silent secret. You move away from a standing start in an unbroken stride of power. And Powerglide now brings you even greater durability. Teamed with the EconoMiser axle and either the new 136-h.p. six or the great new V8, it's optional on all models at extra cost.

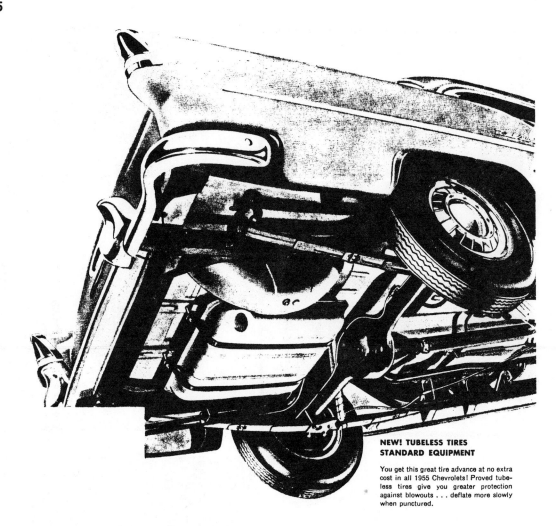

NEW! TUBELESS TIRES STANDARD EQUIPMENT

You get this great tire advance at no extra cost in all 1955 Chevrolets! Proved tubeless tires give you greater protection against blowouts . . . deflate more slowly when punctured.

COMPLETELY NEW 1955 CHEVROLET CHASSIS

The 1955 Chevrolet is just as new underneath as it is "topside"! This completely new chassis is what makes driving the new Chevrolet such a wonderfully exciting experience. You'll find it brings you an entirely new feeling of stability and safety on the road . . . a minimum of pitch and roll on curves . . . almost unbelievable riding smoothness that makes back roads seem like boulevards! And with all its new nimbleness and big-car comfort, the new Chevrolet is every bit as dependable as you've come to expect a Chevrolet to be. In fact, it's designed to deliver a long lifetime of fine performance with even less maintenance than the thrifty Chevrolets of recent years.

NEW HOTCHKISS DRIVE

Drive line shocks are cushioned by new, longer rear springs with Chevrolet's new Hotchkiss Drive. Also, unsprung weight is substantially reduced. Both these factors are important reasons behind Chevrolet's wonderful new ride.

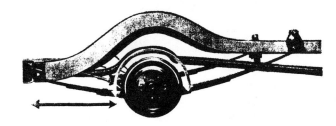

NEW KNEE-ACTION FRONT SUSPENSION

It's the greatest advance in riding comfort since Chevrolet's original Unitized Knee-Action! Four self-adjusting spherical joints absorb road shocks to help give you a wonderfully new kind of ride. And they require much less lubrication!

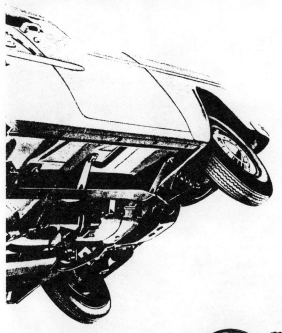

NEW ANTI-DIVE BRAKING CONTROL

This exclusive new Chevrolet development means "heads up" stops—even when you stop in a hurry. It greatly reduces passenger-pitching braking dive. And it lessens chances of bumper locking when you stop in close quarters.

NEW BRAKE ADVANCES

Chevrolet's famed extra-large brakes with bonded linings are even finer for '55! Hydraulic master cylinder is located under the hood for greater servicing ease. Use of nylon bushings in pedal linkage eliminates need for lubrication.

LOWER CENTER OF GRAVITY, WIDER FRONT TREAD

Here are two more important reasons behind the '55 Chevrolet's steady, road-hugging ride. The front tread is 1.3 inches wider. The center of gravity has been substantially lowered. The new Chevrolet is so stable that it requires no front-end stabilizing bar!

NEW ENGINE SUPPORTS

A newly designed engine mounting system cushions engine vibrations and power impulses with greater effectiveness. Live rubber mounts in front and rear support the engine in a naturally balanced position to give you silk-smooth performance at all engine speeds.

THE "TWO-TEN"

SERIES

THE "TWO-TEN" 2-DOOR SEDAN

You can tell just by looking that there's plenty of sports car spirit in
this exciting "Two-Ten" 2-Door Sedan. Notice the dramatic curve of
its Sweep-Sight Windshield . . . its low "let's go" lines. Imagine—all
this glamour in a car that's priced so low!

THE INTERIOR

Seated behind that wheel, you can see all four fenders. And wherever
you sit, you'll enjoy the fashionable two-tone upholstery and smart,
new appointments of this beautifully color-keyed interior.

ENGINEERING SPECIFICATIONS

CAR EXTERIOR DIMENSIONS

Sedans and Coupes: Overall length, 195.6". Overall width, 74.0". Loaded height, 60.5" (Sport Coupe and Convertible, 59.1"). Station Wagons: Overall length, 197.1". Overall width, 74.0". Loaded height, 60.8".

POWER PLANT

Engine: 6-cylinder or 8-cylinder, high-compression, valve-in-head engine in choice of three power teams. Specifications listed below and in the center chart.

Pistons: Tin-coated aluminum alloy, with expansion-controlling steel struts, offset pins, and three rings.

Crankshaft: Precision-counterbalanced, forged steel. Rubber-floated harmonic balancer. Alloy iron camshaft.

Bearings: Precision interchangeable steel-backed babbit crankshaft, camshaft, and connecting rod bearings.

Lubrication: Controlled full-pressure system. Floating oil intake. Crankcase ventilator. Refill, 5 qt. (V8, 4 qt.). Capacity, 16 qt. (17 qt. with heater).

Fuel System: Downdraft carburetion. Automatic choke. Oil-wetted air cleaner. Thermostatic fuel mixture heat control. High-turbulence combustion chambers. 16-gallon tank (17, station wagons) with self-cleaning filter screen. Fuel filler inside of left rear fender, concealed by door.

Exhaust System: 30" reverse-flow muffler with three resonance chambers. Special 24" muffler for Convertible.

Cooling System: Ribbed cellular radiator with pressure cap. 4-blade fan and self-adjusting permanently lubricated water pump. Thermostat and by-pass temperature control. Full-length water jackets around all cylinders.

SUSPENSION SYSTEM

Frame and Bumpers: Double-drop box-girder frame (with special X-structure of I-beams in Convertible). Contoured wraparound bumpers, with guards.

Front Suspension: Independent coil spring suspension, with coaxial life-sealed double-acting shock absorbers. Self-adjusting spherical-joint steering knuckles with non-metallic bearings. Four lubrication fittings.

Rear Suspension: Semi-elliptic leaf springs, 58" long by 2" wide. Lubrication-eliminating leaf inserts. Outrigger mounting, with compression shackles. Diagonally mounted life-sealed double-acting shock absorbers.

Wheels and Tires: Short-spoke steel disk wheels; 5" rims. Full wheel disks on Bel Air models. 6.70-15-4 p.r. extra-low-pressure tubeless tires, others. Wheelbase, 115". Front tread, 58". Rear tread, 58.8".

CONTROLS

Brakes: Hydraulic, self-energizing, with bonded linings. 11" dia. drums with cast alloy iron braking surfaces. Braking dive controlled by car suspension system. Mechanical actuation of rear brakes for parking.

Steering: Recirculating ball-nut steering gear; ratio 20 to 1. Relay type linkage. Overall ratio, 25.7 to 1.

Driving Controls: 18" steering wheel (3-spoke on Bel Air models; 2-spoke on others). Full-circle horn ring on Bel Air and "Two-Ten" models; horn button on "One-Fifty" models. Transmission and direction signal* control levers, with mechanism inside steering column. Parking brake T-handle at left of steering column. Suspended brake and clutch pedals. Treadle accelerator. Foot-controlled headlight-beam switch. Light switch. Key-turn starter and ignition lock switch. Windshield wiper and ventilation controls.

Instruments: Speedometer. Fuel gauge. Heat indicator. Generator charge, oil pressure, and country beam warning lights. Direction signal* arrows. Adjustable indirect instrument lighting. Lighted automatic transmission* selector indicator on instrument panel.

Vision Aids: Two windshield wipers. Full-width defrosting. Inside mirror. Two sun shades (one, "One-Fifty"). Windshield wiper and

Driving Lights: Sealed beam headlights, protected by dual circuit breakers. Parking lights. Tail and stop light units, with red reflex buttons. Dual rear license lights.

BODY CONSTRUCTION

Structure: Welded steel. Turret top with central bow (except Convertible). Full-length floor. Double-walled cowl. Unitized sides and rear fenders. Lacquer finish.

Closures: Rear-opening double-walled doors: Concealed hinges; swing-out type front door hinges. Door checks. Rotary locks. Pushbutton outside handles; lever inside controls. Button-on-sill latches, with rear door safety adjustment. Aluminum sill plates. Two-panel sedan or coupe deck lid: Concealed counterbalancing hinges, key release, lift handle, slam latch. Extra-low trunk sill. Box-section station wagon lift gate: Double-walled station latching supports, wedge lock. Double-walled station wagon tail gate: Exposed hinges, support cables with re-wind springs, slam latches operated by outside T-handle. Key locks for both front doors, deck lid or end gates. Front-opening hood: Counterbalancing hinges, slam latch with safety catch. Convertible folding fabric top: Zippered-in rear curtain with vinyl plastic window, vinyl boot, hydraulic operating mechanism.

Insulation: Thorough sealing and insulation. Extra top sound deadener in Bel Air and "Two-Ten" models.

Front Ventilation: High-level air intake in top of cowl, individually controlled outlets in cowl side panels.

Mounting: Rubber cushioned (except Convertible). Stabilized mounting of front fenders, hood and radiator.

BODY EQUIPMENT

Windows: Polished safety plate glass in windshield and all windows. Windshield: One-piece wraparound; vertical pillars. Door windows: Crank-down. Crank-up of front door ventipanes. Rear quarter windows: Crank-down (2-door sedans, coupes). Stationary (4-door sedans, Utility Sedan). Wraparound stationary (station wagons) with crank-down front sections ("Two-Ten" 2-door model). Rear window: Wraparound (sedans, coupes except Convertible). Curved (station wagons).

Seats: Full-width; all-steel frames with S-wire springs. Front seat: Solid back (4-door models); split center-fold back (2-door models). Foam rubber cushion (Bel Air and "Two-Ten" models). Inclined-plane seat adjustment. Rear seat: Foam rubber cushion (Bel Air and "Two-Ten" sedans, coupes). Folding seat (station wagons).

Upholstery and Trim: All vinyl (Convertible, Club Coupe, "Two-Ten" and "One-Fifty" station wagons); Club Coupe, Rubber mats (others), also sedan and coupe combinations of pattern cloth, gabardine, vinyl (others). Chrome front seat and side wall moldings (Bel Air and "Two-Ten" models); windshield top and side molding (Convertible); roof bows (Sport Coupe).

Floor Coverings: Carpet (Bel Air sedans, coupes; Club Coupe). Rubber mats (others), also sedan and coupe trunk, tail gate, and surface of folded rear seat (station wagons).

Appointments: Wraparound instrument panel with instrument cluster in front of driver, matching radio grille, and central glove compartment with key lock. Automatic glove compartment light, ash receptacle, and cigarette lighter (Bel Air and "Two-Ten" models) and electric clock (Bel Air and "Two-Ten" models). Four arm rests (Bel Air and "Two-Ten" models, except two in station wagons). Two rear seat ash receptacles (Bel Air and "Two-Ten" 2-door models only). Two assist straps (Bel Air and "Two-Ten" 4-door sedans). Two coat hooks (Bel Air and "Two-Ten" 2-door sedans, Club Coupe). Package shelf (sedans, coupes except Convertible).

Lights: Central dome light (sedans, Club Coupe, station wagons). Two rear corner lights (Sport Coupe). Two courtesy lights under instrument panel (Convertible). Manual control by light switch on instrument panel. Automatic switches at all doors (Bel Air models, "Two-Ten" 2-door models) at front doors ("Two-Ten" 4-door models).

Exterior Chrome: Hood ornament, hood and rear emblems, light bezels, radiator grille, bumpers, ventipane frames, handles, hub caps or wheel disks (all models). "V" on rear fenders (V8 models). Windshield, window sill, rear side, and sash moldings ("Two-Ten" models). Windshield and side window moldings; rear window reveal (except Convertible); windshield pillar moldings; front, sash, and rear side moldings (Bel Air models). Special top and belt moldings, and winged spears replacing sash moldings (Bel Air and "Two-Ten" station wagons).

FACTORY-INSTALLED OPTIONAL EQUIPMENT*

Four-barrel carburetor and dual exhaust system for V8 engines. Overdrive. Automatic transmission, in combination with either 6-cylinder or V8 engine. Low-pedal vacuum-power brakes. Hydraulic power steering. Direction signals. Electric windshield wipers. Tinted safety plate glass. Electric-power window lifts. Electric-power front seat adjustment. Heater and defroster. Air conditioner. Whitewall tires.

*Optional at extra cost.

POWER TEAMS	CONVENTIONAL			OVERDRIVE		AUTOMATIC		
	123-hp Six	162-hp V8		123-hp Six	162-hp V8	136-hp Six	162-hp V8	
Engine Size	235.5 cu. in. displacement. 3.56" bore. 3.94" stroke. 7.5 to 1 compression ratio.	265.0 cu. in. displacement. 3.75" bore. 3.0" stroke. 8.0 to 1 compression ratio.		235.5 cu. in. displacement. 3.56" bore. 3.94" stroke. 7.5 to 1 compression ratio.	265.0 cu. in. displacement. 3.75" bore. 3.0" stroke. 8.0 to 1 compression ratio.	235.5 cu. in. displacement. 3.56" bore. 3.94" stroke. 7.5 to 1 compression ratio.	265.0 cu. in. displacement. 3.75" bore. 3.0" stroke. 8.0 to 1 compression ratio.	
Engine Special Features	Concentric carburetor. 4-bearing crankshaft. Gear drive timing.	Dual carburetor. 5-bearing crankshaft. Chain drive timing.		Concentric carburetor. 4-bearing crankshaft. Gear drive timing.	Dual carburetor. 5-bearing crankshaft. Chain drive timing.	Concentric carburetor. 4-bearing crankshaft. High-lift camshaft. Gear drive timing. Hydraulic valve lifters.	Dual carburetor. 5-bearing crankshaft. Chain drive timing. Hydraulic valve lifters.	
Clutch	9½" dia.	10" dia.		9½" dia.	10" dia.			
Transmission	Heavy-Duty Transmission 3-speed, synchro-mesh, selective gear transmission, with gearshift lever on steering column. Gear Ratios: First . . . . 2.94 to 1 Second . . . . 1.68 to 1 Third . . . . 1.00 to 1 Reverse . . . . 2.94 to 1			Heavy-Duty Transmission plus Overdrive* 3-pinion, planetary gear overdrive, providing automatic fourth speed; gear ratio, 0.71 to 1. Accelerator control. Electric cut-in, through releasing treadle, at approx. 25 mph.; down-shift to direct drive by pressing treadle to floor. Pull-out knob locks out overdrive.		Automatic Transmission* Hydraulic, 3-element torque converter, with planetary gears for reverse and automatic low. Selector lever on steering column. Safety switch in starter circuit. Oil cooler integrated with engine cooling system. Maximum torque converter ratio, 2.1 to 1. Planetary gear ratio, 1.82 to 1. Maximum overall ratio, 3.82 to 1.		
Rear Axle	Semi-floating, with hypoid gears. One-piece "banjo" housing. Hotchkiss drive.							
	3.70 to 1 ratio			4.11 to 1 ratio		3.55 to 1 ratio		

Diaphragm spring type. Life-lubricated throwout bearing. Strap drive.

All illustrations and specifications contained in this literature are based on the latest product information available at the time of publication approval. The right is reserved to make changes at any time without notice in prices, colors, materials, equipment, specifications and models, and also to discontinue models.

CHEVROLET MOTOR DIVISION OF GENERAL MOTORS CORPORATION, DETROIT 2, MICHIGAN

PRINTED IN U.S.A.

Don't argue with this baby!

All the low-priced cars
and most of the high-priced cars
tried it recently in official NASCAR* trials...
and took a licking!

Meet the champ! The new Chevrolet 180-h.p. "Super Turbo-Fire V8" — the most modern V8 on the road today.

You want facts, don't you? And not ours. Facts instead from an independent, outside source where the only thing that counts is who came in first, second, and so on. Here they are —

Daytona Beach. NASCAR Acceleration Tests Over Measured Mile From Standing Start. Chevrolet captured the 4 top positions in its class! 8 of the first 11! And on a time basis Chevrolet beat every high-priced car, too — but one!

Daytona Beach. NASCAR Straightaway Running open to cars delivered in Florida for $2,500 or less. Chevrolet captured the first two places, 7 out of the first 11 places!

Daytona Beach. NASCAR 2-Way Straightaway Running over measured mile. Open to cars from 250 to 299 cu. in. displacement. Chevrolet captured 3 of the first 5 places! None of its competition (What competition?) even finished "in the money"!

Columbia, S. C. NASCAR 100-Mile Race on half-mile track. Very tight turns. Chevrolet finished first! Way, *way* ahead — as in sales! With a new car, and *no* pit stops!

Fayetteville, N. C. NASCAR Late Model Event. After running the fastest qualifying round — (with a new car) — Chevrolet again finished first. Because of even tighter turns the driver chose to run the entire 150 laps in second gear! Yet no overheating or pit stops!

These facts you can't laugh off. Sales Leader, Road Leader, a crowning achievement of Chevrolet and General Motors. *Try* a Chevrolet and live in a land of going-away where you win all the arguments! Today, maybe? . . . Chevrolet Division of General Motors, Detroit 2, Mich.

*National Association for Stock Car Auto Racing

SPECIAL: *Added power for the Chevrolet "Super Turbo-Fire V8" — the new 195-h.p. Special Power Kit now available at extra cost on special order.*

   **SALES LEADER FOR 19 STRAIGHT YEARS**

WHO'S RUNNING NUMBER ONE IN COMPETITION WHERE "CLAIMS" DON'T COUNT?

CHEVROLET ▷

THAT'S WHO!

In NASCAR* Short Track Division events, this '55 Chevrolet has brought home more winning points than any car in any price class. Engine and performance <u>claims</u> don't count in this league. Here you've either got it or you haven't!

*National Association for Stock Car Auto Racing

budget low

Chevrolet's got it! Enough high-powered punch to run the pants off competition—*all competition*, including most of the so-called "hot" high-priced cars!

If you've seen a '55 Chevrolet in action this news doesn't surprise you. You've witnessed the swivel-hipped way it handles, breaking through the pack to come lane-hugging, power-sliding through the turns—wide-spaced rear springs holding tight—then digging out with a catapult surge of V8 power! If you haven't—brother, it's something to see. Better yet, put a new Chevrolet through your own paces. Your dealer has one waiting. . . . Chevrolet Division of General Motors, Detroit 2, Michigan.

*the new winner
in stock car competition*

MOTOR TREND/SEPTEMBER 1955 **13**

CHEVROLET'S TAKING COMPETITION TO THE CLEANERS!

The records prove that in NASCAR Short Track events, '55 Chevrolets have rolled up almost twice as many points as their nearest competitor —really cooling the hot high-priced jobs and clobbering *everything* in their own price class.

Why?

Because the '55 Chevrolet V8 is a lot more than just a plain passenger car! There's real *sports car* handling in the accuracy of its Ball-Race steering, the broad base of its outrigger rear springs, the road grip of its spherical-joint front suspension. These things mean more fun for you behind the wheel—*and safer, surer control wherever you*

drive. You pass, stop, steer and take the turns with new confidence and security.

Look at it from any angle and the 1955 Chevrolet V8 is a lot more car than the low-price field has ever known before. It's easy to see why the 180-horsepower "Super Turbo-Fire"* version (with four-barrel carburetor, big manifold and dual exhausts) is setting the drag strips on fire.

And when you consider the *potential* in that ultra-light, ultra-compact powerplant—well, borrow one from your Chevrolet dealer and we won't have to do any more talking; *this* V8 can speak for itself!

Optional at extra cost.

 CHEVROLET DIVISION OF GENERAL MOTORS, DETROIT 2, MICHIGAN

After the success of its 1955 offerings, Chevrolet was to continue refining the basic styling and design during 1956. Industry sales were off from their 1955 high but Chevrolet would still out pace Ford in total production this year by just under 200,000 units.

The same three series were offered in 1956: the Bel Air, "Two-Ten," and "One-Fifty." These series came in 19 models. The new addition to the model line-up was the pillarless 4-door Sport Hardtop which was available in both the Bel Air and "Two-Ten" lines.

Body changes were limited to trim and detail features. Most notably, a new Chevrolet medallion graced the hood and the side chrome extended in an unbroken line from the rear bumper to just behind the headlights (except on the "One-Fifty"). The grille was new and extended across the whole front of the car incorporating the parking lights.

The big news, as always for these exciting cars, was in the continued developement of the 265 V-8 engine. With the 2-bbl set up, the engine would turn 162-hp at 2200 RPM or 170-hp at 4400 RPM with an 8:1 compression ratio. With the 4-bbl carburetion, it would turn 205-hp at 3000 RPM or 210-hp at 3200 RPM with an 9.25:1 compression ratio. Finally, although listed as a "Corvette V-8", the engine could be modified on any Chvey with dual 4-bbl

carburetors to turn 225-hp at 5200 RPM with a 9.25:1 compression ratio. The durability of this engine was demonstrated when a stock 225-hp sedan averaged a little over 101 mph for 24 hrs. in a race at the track in Darlington, SC.

Wheelbase remained 115" and overall length increased from 195.6" to 197.5" while width decreased from 74" to 73.4". Prices and weights were up. A Bel Air V-8 four-door sedan, for example, weighed 41 lbs. more than in 1955 and cost $136 more. The least expensive Chevrolet was the "One-Fifty" two-door sedan at $1,925 (3,144 lbs.) and the most expensive (excluding station wagons) was the Bel Air Convertible at $2,443 (3,320 lbs.). The Nomad's base price was $2,707 (3,342 lbs.).

Production of "One-Fifty" series was 157,294. Production of "Two-Ten" series was 737,371 and of Bel Air series was 540,682. Nomad production was 7,886 (included in Bel Air production figures also).

Literature this year included the full-line Chevy catalogue (pages 20-21) and a full-line folder. Chevrolet didn't overlook the impact it was having on the track, either. A stock car tie-in piece was issued to dealers advertising a special kit which could be used to advertise Chevy performance in local race meets (pages 22-24). The ritual Pike's Peak climb was also not overlooked in the literature (pages 25-28).

ENGINEERING SPECIFICATIONS

CAR EXTERIOR DIMENSIONS

Sedans and Coupes: Overall length, 197.5". Overall width, 74.0". Loaded height, 60.5" (Sport Coupe, Sport Sedan, and Convertible, 59.1"). **Station Wagons:** Overall length, 200.8". Overall width, 74.0". Loaded height, 60.8".

POWER PLANT

Engine: 6-cylinder or 8-cylinder, high-compression, valve-in-head engine with h.p. ranging up to 225. Specifications listed below and in center chart.

Pistons: Tin-coated aluminum alloy, with expansion-controlling steel struts, offset pins, three rings.

Crankshaft: Precision-counterbalanced, forged steel. Harmonic balancer. Alloy iron camshaft.

Bearings: Precision replaceable steel-backed babbitt (crankshaft, and connecting rods).

Lubrication: Controlled full-pressure system. Fixed oil intake. Oil Filter*. Refill, 5 qt. (V8, 4 qt.).

Fuel System: Downdraft carburetion. Automatic choke. Air cleaner. Thermostatic fuel mixture heat control. High-turbulence combustion chambers. 16-gallon tank (17, station wagons) with filter screen in tank. Fuel filler concealed by left tail light.

Exhaust System: 30" reverse-flow muffler with three resonance chambers. Special 24" muffler for Convertible. Super Turbo-Fire V8 and Corvette V8 have full dual exhaust system.

Cooling System: Ribbed cellular radiator with pressure cap. 4-blade fan and life-lubricated water pump. Thermostat and by-pass temperature control. Full-length water jackets around all cylinders. Capacity, 16 qt. (17 qt. with heater).

Electrical System: 12-volt system. 54-plate battery (53 ampere-hour rating at 20 hours). 25-ampere generator, with current and voltage regulators. Solenoid-actuated positive-shift starter. All-weather ignition. Automatic centrifugal and vacuum spark control.

Mounting: Balanced on rubber cushions.

SUSPENSION SYSTEM

Frame and Bumpers: Double-drop box-girder frame (special X-structure of I-beams in Convertible). Contoured wraparound bumpers, with guards.

Front Suspension: Independent coil spring suspension, with coaxial life-sealed double-acting shock absorbers. Self-adjusting spherical-joint steering knuckles with non-metallic bearings. Four lubrication fittings.

Rear Suspension: Semi-elliptic leaf springs, 58" by 2". Lubrication-eliminating leaf inserts. Outrigger mounting, with compression shackles. Diagonally mounted life-sealed double-acting shock absorbers.

Wheels and Tires: Steel disk wheels; 5" rims. Full wheel disks on Bel Air models; hub caps on others. 6.70-15-4 p.r. extra-low-pressure tubeless tires. 6.70-15-6 p.r. on nine passenger station wagons. Wheelbase, 115". Front tread, 58". Rear tread, 58.8".

CONTROLS

Brakes: Hydraulic, self-energizing, with bonded linings. 11" dia. drums with cast alloy iron braking surfaces. Braking dive controlled by suspension. Mechanical actuation of rear brakes for parking.

Steering: Recirculating ball-nut steering gear; ratio 20 to 1. Relay type linkage. Overall ratio, 25.7 to 1.

Driving Controls: 18" steering wheel (3-spoke on Bel Air models; 2-spoke on others). Full-circle horn ring on Bel Air and "Two-Ten" models; horn button on "One-Fifty" models. Transmission and direction signal control levers, with mechanism inside steering column. Parking brake T-handle at left of steering column. Suspended brake and clutch pedals. Treadle accelerator. Foot-controlled headlight beam switch. Light switch. Key-turn starter and ignition lock switch. Windshield wiper and ventilation controls.

Instruments: Speedometer. Fuel gauge. Heat indicator. Generator charge, oil pressure, and country beam warning lights. Direction signal arrows. Adjustable indirect instrument lighting. Lighted automatic transmission selector indicator on instrument panel.

Vision Aids: Two windshield wipers. Full-width defrosting. Inside mirror. Two sun shades (one, "One-Fifty" models).

Driving Lights: Precision-aimed sealed beam headlights, protected by dual circuit breakers. Parking lights. Tail and stop light units, with red reflex buttons. Dual rear license lights.

BODY CONSTRUCTION

Structure: Welded steel. Turret top with central bow (except Convertible). Station wagons (except Nomad) have two roof bows. Full-length floor. Double-walled cowl. Unitized sides and rear fenders. Lacquer finish.

Closures: Rear-opening double-walled doors: Concealed hinges; swing-out type front door hinges. Door checks. Safety type rotary locks. Pushbutton outside handles; lever inside controls. Button-on-sill locks, with rear door safety adjustment. Aluminum sill plates. Two-panel sedan and coupe deck lid: Concealed torque-rod counterbalancing hinges, key release, lift handle, slam latch. Extra-low trunk sill. Box-section station wagon lift gate: Concealed hinges, self-latching supports, wedge lock. Double-walled station wagon tail gate: Exposed hinges, support cables with re-wind springs, slam latches operated by outside T-handle. Key locks for both front doors, deck lid or end gates. Front-opening hood: Counterbalancing hinges, slam latch with safety catch. Convertible folding fabric top: Zippered-in rear curtain with vinyl plastic window, vinyl boot, hydraulic operating mechanism.

Insulation: Thorough sealing and insulation.

Front Ventilation: High-level air intake in top of cowl; individually controlled outlets in cowl sides.

Mounting: Rubber cushioned (except Convertible). Stabilized front-end mounting.

BODY EQUIPMENT

Windows: High quality safety glass in windshield and all windows. Windshield: One-piece panoramic; vertical pillars. Door windows: Crank-down. Crank-operated front door ventipanes. Rear quarter windows: Crank-down (2-door sedans, coupes). Stationary (4-door sedans, Utility Sedan). Wraparound stationary (station wagons). Wraparound stationary (Bel Air and "Two-Ten" 2-door models) with movable front sections. Rear window: Wraparound (sedans, coupes and station wagons).

Seats: Full-width; steel frames with S-wire springs. Front seat: Solid back (4-door models); split center-fold back (2-door models). Inclined-plane seat adjustment. Rear seat: Foam rubber cushion (Bel Air sedans, coupes and Nomad). Folding seat (six-passenger station wagons). Nine-passenger station wagon: Folding center seat with off-center divided back, removable rear seat.

Upholstery and Trim: All vinyl (Convertible, Club Coupe, "Two-Ten" and "One-Fifty" station wagons); combinations of pattern cloth and vinyl (others). Chrome front seat and side wall moldings (Bel Air and "Two-Ten" models); windshield top and side molding (Convertible). Vinyl headlining (Bel Air Sport Coupe, Sport Sedan, Nomad).

Floor Coverings: Carpet (Bel Air sedans, coupes, Nomad, "Two-Ten" coupes). Rubber mats (others), also sedan and coupe trunk, Utility Sedan load space. Linoleum on platform, tail gate, and surface of folded rear seat (station wagons).

Appointments: Wraparound instrument panel with instrument cluster in front of driver, matching

---

All illustrations and specifications contained in this literature are based on the latest product information available at the time of publication approval. The right is reserved to make changes at any time without notice in prices, colors, materials, equipment, specifications and models, and also to discontinue models.

PRINTED IN U.S.A.—2   **CHEVROLET MOTOR DIVISION OF GENERAL MOTORS CORPORATION, DETROIT 2, MICHIGAN**   *Optional at extra cost.

Bel Air 4-Door Sedan

radio grille, ashtray and central glove compartment with key lock. Automatic glove compartment light, ashtray on instrument panel on all jobs, and cigarette lighter (Bel Air and "Two-Ten" models) and electric clock (Bel Air models). Four arm rests (Bel Air and "Two-Ten" models, except two in station wagons). Two rear seat ash receptacles (Bel Air and "Two-Ten" 2-door models; one, Bel Air and "Two-Ten" 4-door sedans. Two assist straps (Bel Air and "Two-Ten" 2-door sedans, Club Coupe). Package shelf (sedans, coupes except Convertible).

Lights: Central dome light. Two courtesy lights under instrument panel (Convertible), two lights in Nomad. Manual switch on instrument panel. Automatic switches at all doors (Bel Air models); at front doors ("Two-Ten" models).

Exterior Chrome: Hood ornament, hood and rear emblems, light bezels, grille, bumpers, ventipane frames, handles, hub caps or wheel disks. "V" on hood and rear deck (V8 models). V's on Nomad rear fenders. Windshield, rear window, side, and sash moldings ("Two-Ten" and "One-Fifty" models), window sill ("Two-Ten" models). Windshield and side window moldings; rear window reveal (except Convertible); windshield pillar moldings; sash and double side moldings (Bel Air models). Special top and belt moldings (Bel Air and "Two-Ten" station wagons).

FACTORY-INSTALLED OPTIONAL EQUIPMENT*

Overdrive. Automatic transmission. Heavy-duty oil bath air cleaner (all 6-cylinder models). Heavy-duty clutch. Low-pedal vacuum-power brakes. Hydraulic power steering. Electric windshield wipers. Tinted safety glass. Electric-power window lifts. Electric-power front seat adjustment. Heater and defroster. Air conditioner. Whitewall tires. Six ply tires. Heavy-duty rear springs.

POWER TEAMS	CONVENTIONAL	OVERDRIVE	AUTOMATIC
Blue-Flame 140	Valve-in-head 140-h.p. Six-cylinder engine. 235.5 cubic inch displacement. 3.56" bore, 3.94" stroke, 8.0 to 1 compression ratio. Concentric carburetor, 4-bearing crankshaft, gear-drive timing, hydraulic valve lifters.		
Turbo-Fire V8	Valve-in-head 162-h.p. (170-h.p. with Powerglide) V8 engine. 265 cubic inch displacement. 3.75" bore, 3.0" stroke, 8.0 to 1 compression ratio. Two-barrel carburetor. 5-bearing crankshaft, chain-drive timing, hydraulic valve lifters. Heavy-duty oil-bath air cleaner.		
Super Turbo-Fire V8	Valve-in-head 205-h.p. V8 engine. 265 cubic inch displacement. 3.75" bore, 3.0" stroke, 9.25 to 1 compression ratio. Four-barrel carburetor, 5-bearing crankshaft, chain-drive timing, hydraulic valve lifters, heavy-duty oil-bath air cleaner, dual exhaust system.		
Corvette V8	Valve-in-head V8 engine. 225 h.p. at 5200 rpm; torque, 270 ft-lbs at 3600 rpm. 265 cubic inch displacement. 3.75" bore, 3.0" stroke, 9.25 to 1 compression ratio. Dual four-barrel carburetors, two oil-bath air cleaners, special high-lift camshaft, high-speed mechanical valve lifters, high-power exhaust headers, dual exhaust system.		
Clutch	Diaphragm spring type with permanently lubricated throw-out bearing. 9½" diameter on Six; 10" diameter on Turbo-Fire V8. Coil spring type, 10" diameter on Super Turbo-Fire V8 and Corvette V8.		None
Transmission	Heavy-Duty Transmission 3-speed, synchro-mesh selective gear transmission, with gearshift lever on steering column. Gear Ratios: First..........2.94 to 1 Second........1.68 to 1 Third..........1.00 to 1 Reverse.......2.94 to 1	Heavy-Duty Transmission plus Overdrive* 3-pinion, planetary gear overdrive, providing automatic fourth speed; gear ratio, 0.71 to 1. Accelerator control: Electric cut-in, through releasing treadle, above 30 mph.; down-shift to direct drive by pressing treadle to floor. Pull-out knob locks out overdrive.	Automatic Transmission* Hydraulic, 3-element torque converter, with planetary gears for reverse and low. Selector lever on steering column. Safety switch in starter circuit. Oil cooler integrated with engine cooling system. Maximum torque converter ratio, 2.1 to 1. Planetary gear ratio, 1.82 to 1. Maximum overall ratio, 3.82 to 1.
Rear Axle	Semi-floating, with hypoid gears. Single-unit "banjo" housing. Hotchkiss drive.		
	3.70 to 1 ratio	4.11 to 1 ratio	3.55 to 1 ratio

Bel Air Nomad

Here's what's happening on stock car tracks

Chevrolet Scores Big News In Stock Car Racing

● The hot one's even hotter in '56! Chevrolet is sweeping to victory in NASCAR's* torrid short track circuit, piling up more than twice as many points as its nearest competitor. The '56 season is only a few months old and already Chevrolet is demonstrating its superb performance not only in Short Track competition but also in Grand National and Convertible races.**

Chevrolet's victory list includes important wins at Fayetteville, Los Angeles, Hollywood, Fla., Fresno, Virginia Beach, and Atlanta, Ga. And Chevrolet, as you know, won the acceleration and flying mile runs in its class at Daytona—for the *second* year. All of these outstanding victories are record-book proof for your prospects that Chevrolet has the top V8 in the low-price field!

This tremendous story means that Chevrolet is carrying on where it left off in 1955, when the car won NASCAR's Short Track championship by a whopping margin of 473 points. Chevrolet scored headline news last year at the Daytona Time Trials where it won the acceleration and flying mile events for its class. After this sensational showing, many leading professional race drivers switched to Chevrolet because it had the necessary qualities to win on the track.

Then came important wins in '55 at Fayetteville, Atlanta, Jersey City, Chicago, Cedar Rapids—to name

only a few victory towns—establishing Chevrolet as a consistent winner in stock car racing. And the '55 season was capped with Chevrolet's victory in the "World Series of Stock Car Racing"—the Darlington 500.

Chevrolet provides Dealers with advertising and promotional support

National newspaper ads headlined Chevrolet's stock car racing victories throughout 1955. A hard-hitting promotional campaign including window trim, salesmen's folders, hand-out pieces, and the Stock Car Plans Book were prepared last year to help you tell Chevrolet's blistering performance story.

This same success story is being heralded again in national advertising during '56—giving solid backing to your sales talks with prospects.

A consistent sales promotion campaign continues to keep you informed of the car's current success on stock car tracks. A special salesmen's folder was sent to you when Chevrolet scored two wins early this racing season. To help you capitalize on Chevrolet's victories in NASCAR's time trials at Daytona Beach this year, you were furnished with window trim, an official results folder and the *Daytona Beach Story.* Chevrolet's Stock Car Racing News Reports keep you up to date on the latest triumphs in competition. And now the '56 Stock Car Racing Promotion Kit is ready to help you tie in with a local race.

Chevrolet dealers everywhere benefit from all of this concentrated advertising and promotional activity because it's another way to demonstrate vividly Chevrolet's product superiority.

National Association for Stock Car Auto Racing.

**NASCAR breaks down its racing classifications according to track lengths: Short Track races are held on tracks less than a half mile long; Grand National races on tracks ½ mile or over; Convertible races are run on both kinds of tracks.*

OFFICIAL NASCAR SHORT TRACK STANDINGS			
1955		1956 (As of April 28, 1956)	
1. CHEVROLET	668	1. CHEVROLET	226
2. OLDSMOBILE	195	2. FORD	91
3. HUDSON	184	3. DODGE	47
4. DODGE	176	4. MERCURY	38
5. FORD	165	5. PONTIAC	12
6. PLYMOUTH	115	6. PLYMOUTH	11
7. MERCURY	92	7. HUDSON	10
8. CHRYSLER	46	8. OLDSMOBILE	5

Tie in with Chevrolet's stock car racing program!

You can use a stock car race to build community excitement that leads to sales

Stock car racing commands attention from performance-minded prospects. Proof of Chevrolet's product superiority comes alive when the car roars to victory and *you tell the story*.

By identifying your dealership with a local race, you'll attract more prospects and showroom traffic. Chevrolet's 1956 Stock Car Racing Plans Book is designed to show you how to do it *successfully*—and the kit contains colorful materials to do a great job of building enthusiasm for Chevrolet. The materials in the kit are shown on the back page of this folder.

Even if you have no opportunity to tie in with a race, you still benefit from Chevrolet's stock car success. Chevrolet's winning story is timely anywhere in the country—and the car's performance, as proved in stock car races, helps you strengthen your sales talks.

Here's how one dealer capitalizes on stock car racing

C. V. Nalley, Inc., Chevrolet Dealer in Gainesville, Georgia, has found that tying in with local stock car races produces sales results! In addition, Nalley sponsors a driver in many stock car races in the area. Thousands of people who attend the stock car races see Nalley's name prominently painted on the side of the car—another attention-getter for the dealership. Following each race he displays the Chevrolet on a turntable in his showroom.

This special display attracts hundreds of people to his dealership creating showroom traffic which has resulted in additional sales.

Left to right: Logan Nalley, Chevrolet Dealer; Chester Barron, Stock Car Driver; Cuz Bell, Nalley Sales Manager.

You can turn stock car racing results into sales for you. Next to a personal demonstration drive for a prospect, there's no better way to prove Chevrolet's superior performance than when it flashes down the track to victory ahead of all competition!

Chevrolet has available a special kit to help dealers who want to tie in with local stock car races

● Here's the line-up of promotional aids that Chevrolet has made available to help dealers tie in with a local race and do an all-round job of building local interest in the '56 Chevrolet.

WINDOW TRIM

TWO NEWSPAPER ADS

TRUNK BANNER AND PACE CAR DOOR BANNER

TWO PUBLICITY RELEASES
TWO RADIO SPOTS

1956 CHEVROLET OFFICIALLY BREAKS PIKES PEAK RECORD

Run timed and governed by rigid NASCAR* rules

*National Association for Stock Car Auto Racing

INSPECTED AND READY TO GO

An official inspection team headed by Bill France, President of NASCAR, thoroughly checked the 1956 pre-production model Chevrolet to make sure it conformed to 1956 stock car specifications. Zora Arkus-Duntov, famous European competition driver and Chevrolet engineer, drove the new record breaker.

STARTER'S FLAG WAVES "GO"

And, this new 1956 Chevrolet . . . camouflaged under plastic hoods and striped with black . . . powered by the new 205-hp "Super Turbo-Fire V8" . . . charged across the starting line.

CHALLENGE AHEAD

There it was . . . Pikes Peak road, 12.42 miles long and a famous automotive proving ground. The course begins near 7-mile point, 9402 feet above sea level, and it bends through a series of 170 curves to the finish line at the top, 14,110 feet high.

NO OTHER CAR HAS SO

PIKES PEAK TEST IS PROOF OF 1956 CHEVROLET'S OUTSTANDING PERFORMANCE THAT MEANS GREATER SAFETY FOR YOU

You'll never have to experience this thrill-filled ride that flirted with danger . . . steep grades . . . hairpin turns . . . narrow bumpy roads along the side of precipitous cliffs . . . as this powerful new 1956 Chevrolet did when it set a new all-time speed record for stock cars on the Pikes Peak run. It took just 17 minutes, 24:05 seconds to zoom up the 12.42 miles. And that shattered the old Pikes Peak record by more than 2 full minutes.

But you'll want the extra safety of driving a 1956 Chevrolet. And it took this record to prove conclusively that outstanding performance means greater safety . . . and it's built right into this new Chevrolet. It showed beyond doubt that the 1956 Chevrolet guarantees better passenger safety with faster acceleration for quicker passing . . . easy, smooth cornering ability . . . greater stability for a smooth, low, road-hugging ride.

SAFE . . . ROCK-STEADY CORNERING
Any severe, hairpin turns on the Pikes Peak record run fully proved the amazing cornering ability the 1956 Chevrolet. It took them all in stride, in complete safety, because Chevrolet has *unique trigger rear springs* that give superior cornering qualities.

SAFE, TRIGGER-QUICK ACCELERATION
Chevrolet's new 205-horsepower "Super Turbo-Fire V8" is in a class all its own when it comes to "get-up-and-go." It had to be to set the new Pikes Peak record. This surging power delivers safe, steady acceleration at the slightest touch. And, when you need it for quick passing, Chevrolet's got a quick, lightning power reserve to draw on.

PERMANENT STAMINA
Each twisting, tortuous, curving foot of the 12.42-mile Pikes Peak climb challenged this 1956 Chevrolet to prove its stamina and durability under driving conditions far in excess of what most motorists encounter. And as the record shows, it passed this rugged test—with plenty to spare.

SAFE . . . SURE-FOOTED ROADABILITY
Rolling along at record speed, the 1956 Chevrolet, with its low center of gravity, hugged Pikes Peak's rocky road snugly. Its *ball-Race steering*, pioneered in the low-price field by Chevrolet, provided steering ease and precision control. And its *Glide-Ride front suspension* smoothed out the "rock and roll" motion.

EVER GONE SO HIGH FAST – SO SAFELY!

TIMING

"The 12.42-mile distance was covered in 17 minutes, 24.05 seconds for a new record for American stock sedans," reported Bill France, President of NASCAR. Joe Epton (at right), official timer for the test, set up the sensitive timing devices used.

SAFE . . . EFFORTLESS TURNING

No other car has ever gone so high, so fast, so safely . . . *and taken so many turns* at high speed as the 1956 Chevrolet did on Pikes Peak. Chevrolet's *Ball-Race steering* gave pin-point steering accuracy with a minimum of effort—and coupled with *Glide-Ride front suspension* and *outrigger rear springs*, no turn was too tough. It won't be for you either in a 1956 Chevrolet with its greater safety.

SAFE . . . PEAK LEVELING POWER

It took plenty of staying power to set a new Pikes Peak record. And the marvelous Chevrolet "Turbo-Fire" engine, with its 1956 improvements, was equal to the challenge. It is extremely well balanced with capacity to build up and maintain high engine R.P.M. And, its excellent cooling system kept the car from overheating.

SAFE . . . ANTI-DIVE BRAKING

Not much braking was done on this record run . . . but it was there, reliably so, in Jumbo size. *Anti-Dive braking control,* an exclusive Chevrolet feature that counteracts "nosing down" during normal braking, gives "heads-up" stops even when you stop in a hurry.

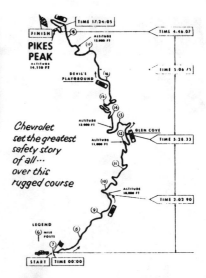

*Chevrolet
set the greatest
safety story
of all...
over this
rugged course*

NEAR THE TOP

As Chevrolet's Pikes Peak record breaker hit the last leg of its climb, driver Arkus-Duntov really poured it on. The test was run early in the morning before this famous skyline drive was open to the public. At this point near the finish line, the car literally "blurred" its way uphill.

A NEW PIKES PEAK CHAMP

The checkered flag waved down as the new champion swept across the finish line to cut more than two minutes from the standard passenger car record of 19 minutes, 25:70 seconds. In addition to official starters, timers and other experts from NASCAR, the record run was witnessed by E. G. (Cannonball) Baker, National Commissioner for stock car racing and former holder of the Pikes Peak record.

CONGRATULATIONS TO THE VICTOR

After the timing devices proclaimed the new record, Zora Arkus-Duntov was congratulated by NASCAR officials. And Pikes Peak, long recognized as a rugged proving grounds for testing the acceleration, roadability and handling characteristics of automotive products . . . had a new champion . . . the 1956 Chevrolet.

DRIVE THE PIKES PEAK RECORD BREAKER TODAY!

Put yourself behind the wheel of a Pikes Peak Record Breaker. Enjoy its smooth acceleration, its easy handling and its greater riding comfort.

This would be the year that would mark the end of Chevrolet's "modern classic" era. It was also a year of furious competition between Ford and Chevrolet for the title of "No. 1 Auto producer." It was a battle that Ford would win on model year production but Chevrolet would win (by a nose) on a calendar year production basis. There should be no question in anyone's mind, however, that Chevrolet set the performance standard with the introduction of the revolutionary fuel-injected V-8.

The 1957 Chevrolet, today, is one of the most sought after cars of the postwar period. The new grille, the "machine gun" hood ornamentation, the revised hood medallion, the vestigal finning of the rear quarter panel all combined to achieve a beautiful package. Contemporary Nomad buyers, however, apparently didn't completely agree with latter-day enthusiasts. Only 6,103 were built in this the Nomad's last year as a distinct model.

As always with these great cars, the major story was under the hood. This was the year that Chevrolet achieved the one-horsepower-per-cubic-inch goal by boring out a 265 V-8 to 283 cubic inches which, with Ram fuel-injection, would turn out 283-hp at 6200 RPM. Chevrolet offered a total of seven V-8 engine options. Bottom of the line was the 265 V-8 with 162-hp at 4400 RPM with 2-bbl carburetion. Next up was the 283 V-8 with 185-hp at 4600 RPM and 8.5:1 compression or 220-hp at 4800 RPM with 9.5:1 compression with 4-bbl carburetion. With dual 4-bbl carbs the 283 would turn out 245-hp at 5000 RPM or 270-hp at 6000 RPM with 9.5:1 compression. Fuel-injection would buy you 250-hp at 5000 RPM with a 9.5:1 compression ratio or 283-hp at 6200 RPM with a 10.5:1 compression ratio. With the 283-hp version you could also get the close-ratio 3-speed Synchro-Mesh transmission.

The least expensive Chevrolet was the "One-Fifty" two-door sedan at $2,096 (3,207 lbs.) and the most expensive (excluding station wagons) was the Bel Air Convertible at $2,611 (3,405 lbs.). A two-door Bel Air was $2,338 (3,228 lbs.) and a two-door "Two-Ten" was base priced at $2,222 (3,221 lbs.). Production of "One-Fifty" models was 153,353, "Two-Ten" models was 653,358 and of Bel Air models was 702,220.

Literature issued this year included the full-line Chevrolet catalogue (pages 32-34) and the full-line folder (cover shown below). Again, there was a series of magazine ads extolling Chevy performance (pages 30-31 and 35-38).

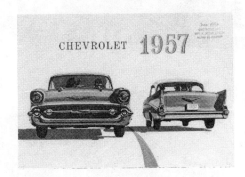

This is the car that's fresher and friskier from its own special look to its new Ram-jet fuel injection!

Those words—sweet, smooth and sassy—seem to fit this new Chevy right down to its tubeless tires. In the first place, it *looks* the part. It has a crisp, alert appearance—as trim and functional as an arrow. You can tell that the styling isn't just going along for the ride. It's right in keeping with Chevrolet's own special fresh and frisky ways.

And this is one car that looks as good close up as it does across the street. It's built the way you've come to expect a Chevrolet to be built. Everything in it fits beautifully —including you!

But a Chevy isn't just something

sweet (just look!) *smooth* (ah, that Turboglide!)

June 8, 1957

that's nice to look at. Far from it. This beauty was meant for *driving*—and it *knows* it! Give a Chevrolet a gentle hint with your toe, and it responds with spunk and spirit and sureness!

You can pick your power from the widest choice of engines in Chevy's field—from the popular Chevy 6 up to V8's with revolutionary Ramjet fuel injection.* This Chevy advance does away with the carburetor . . . brings you instant responsiveness and more efficient use of fuel. It's the greatest forward step in engines since overhead valves!

When you put Chevrolet's new Turboglide* drive in the picture, you're really living! It's the first and only triple-turbine transmission.

Get your hands on the sweetest handling car of them all. It's as close by as your nearest Chevrolet dealer's. . . . Chevrolet Division of General Motors, Detroit 2, Michigan.

Optional at extra cost.

The Bel Air Convertible with Body by Fisher (at left, below). The Chevrolet Corvette (at right).

sassy (just drive it!)

*Extra-cost option

THE "SUPER TURBO-FIRE 283"

A NEW PEAK IN SMOOTH V8 PERFORMANCE!

In its advanced new short-stroke "Super Turbo-Fire 283,"* Chevrolet announces headline power news for '57! This mighty V8 delivers high-compression horse-power and husky torque. Big-bore 283-cubic-inch displacement and ultra high 9.5 to 1 compression ratio in the "Super Turbo-Fire 283" deliver a new peak in efficiency. Add balanced 4-barrel carburetion . . . new high lift camshaft . . . Fire Swirl combustion chamber design . . . new ram's horn exhaust headers and dual exhausts . . . new unitized starter . . . plus other advanced features—and you have America's newest and best power buy for 1957. What's more, it is available in all passenger car models and with your choice of four great transmissions.

NEW! "CORVETTE V8" *with fuel injection*

Here's even greater performance—two powerful versions of the special "Cor-vette V8"* engine, available in all passenger car models for 1957! One version gives you extra power using twin 4-barrel carburetors—the other offers you Chevrolet's trend-starting new fuel injection, most far-reaching engine improve-ment in the entire industry! With the carburetor completely eliminated, fuel injection results in the most instantaneously responsive power you've ever known . . . and a brand new measure of fuel efficiency!

"TURBO-FIRE 283"
"TURBO-FIRE 265"

V8 POWER AT LOW COST!

For '57 Chevrolet announces two lower cost versions of "Turbo-Fire" design—engineered for economical V8 performance, high torque and horsepower. The 283-cu.-in. "Turbo-Fire 283,"* with 8.5 to 1 compression ratio, is available in all models with automatic drive. Its running mate, the "Turbo-Fire 265" has a 265-cu.-in. displacement, 8.0 to 1 compression ratio and is available in all models equipped with Powerglide, Overdrive or Synchro-Mesh transmissions. *All* V8's are of Chevrolet's famous short-stroke valve-in-head design. All are precision balanced in assembly, *extra* light, *extra* rigid, *extra* compact—built to the road-proved design that makes Chevrolet so well balanced and maneuverable, so much fun to go in!

... THE POWER TEAM OF YOUR CHOICE

All power teams available in all **Bel Air**, **"Two-Ten"** and **"One-Fifty"** models. See your Chevrolet dealer for the price of the power team you prefer.	Turboglide	Powerglide	Overdrive	Synchro-Mesh*
"Corvette V8" 283-cu.-in. V8, 9.5:1 c.r. Twin 4-barrel carburetion**	●	●	●	●
"Super Turbo-Fire 283" 283-cu.-in. V8, 9.5:1 c.r. Single 4-barrel carburetion	●	●	●	●
"Turbo-Fire 283" 283-cu.-in. V8, 8.5:1 c.r. 2-barrel carburetion	●	●		
"Turbo-Fire 265" 265-cu.-in. V8, 8.0:1 c.r. 2-barrel carburetion		●	●	●
"Blue-Flame" 235-cu.-in. Six, 8.0:1 c.r. Single-barrel carburetion		●	●	●

*Choice of regular Synchro-Mesh or special close-ratio 3-speed available with "Corvette V8" engine only.

**Fuel injection system also available with all transmissions except Overdrive.

All Chevrolet engines feature highly efficient valve-in-head design, aluminum pistons, automatic choke, positive-shift starter, forged steel crankshaft, 12-volt electrical system, full pressure lubrication. Full dual exhaust system standard on "Corvette V8" and "Super Turbo-Fire 283." Hydraulic valve lifters on all power teams shown above. Maximum performance version of "Corvette V8" available with close-ratio Synchro-Mesh only on special order features fuel injection system, 9.5 to 1 compression ratio, competition-type camshaft, and high-speed valve system with special valve springs, spring dampers, and mechanical valve lifters.

LUXURY—IN AND OUT

All 1957 Chevrolet models are available in a wide range of exterior colors in either solid tone or two-tone combinations, with distinctive two-tone interiors keyed to exterior color. Your Chevrolet dealer can show you all these exciting exterior colors and actual samples of every fine fabric and costly vinyl interior material.

Bel Air Series—the ultimate in luxury, with gold anodized aluminum grille screen and decorative accents. Ribbed two-tone silver anodized aluminum panel on rear fender and bright metal body sill molding are optional at extra cost. Seven two-tone interiors keyed to exterior color.

"Two-Ten" and "One-Fifty" Series feature silver anodized aluminum grille screen and bright metal decorative accents. Three two-tone interiors, keyed to exterior color. "One-Fifty" sedan interior harmonizes with exterior color. Handyman offers two two-tone interiors, keyed to exterior color.

EXTRA SAFETY ALL AROUND

Rugged all-steel body structure with unitized side panels, double-walled doors, triple-safe door latches, welded-in instrument panel, and central roof bow on all closed models. High quality polished lacquer finish. Convenient single key lock system. High volume ventilation system with air inlets above headlights. Counterbalanced hood with positive safety latch. Concealed deck lid hinges. Hydraulic-powered top on convertible.

FIRM FOUNDATION

Extra-rigid welded box girder frame (special center X in convertible). Glide-Ride front suspension with independent coil springs, low-friction spherical joints, and exclusive anti-dive braking action. Outrigger rear suspension, with extra-long permanently lubricated leaf springs. Life-sealed double-acting shock absorbers. Luxury-cushion 7.50-14 4-ply (6-ply on 9-passenger station wagon) tubeless tires. Powerful hydraulic self-energizing Jumbo-Drum brakes with 11" drums and bonded linings. Mechanical parking brake on both rear wheels. Exclusive Ball-Race steering gear with balanced linkage. Proved 12-volt electrical system, 54-plate battery with 36-month warranty. Precision-aimed sealed beam headlights. Built-in directional signals. Rear axle ratio matched to power team: Synchro-Mesh, 3.55:1; Overdrive, 4.11:1; Powerglide and Turboglide, 3.36:1. Fuel tank capacity: station wagons, 17 gallons; other models, 16 gallons.

MEASURES OF QUALITY

Wheelbase, 115". Front tread 58.0", rear tread, 58.8". Overall dimensions: length 202.8"; width 73.9"; loaded height 60.5" (sport coupe, sport sedan, convertible 59.1", station wagons 60.8").

THESE ARE OPTIONAL AT EXTRA COST

Power steering. Power brakes. Power windows. Power front seat. E-Z-Eye glass. Padded instrument panel. Heater. Air Conditioner. Electric windshield wipers. White sidewall tires (rayon or nylon cord). Heavy-duty 6-ply tires. Heavy-duty clutch, heavy-duty rear springs, and other mechanical features. Safety belt, shoulder harness, choice of radios, and full range of other accessory equipment.

AND IN PRICE ...

Chevrolet is traditionally America's lowest priced line of quality automobiles. See your Chevrolet dealer for the exact delivered price of the model of your choice, equipped as you like it.

CHEVY COMES TO THE LINE <u>LOADED</u> FOR '57!

RAMJET <u>FUEL INJECTION</u>!* Did you ever think you'd see this first in the low-price field? Constant-flow fuel injection . . . with instant acceleration that *sprints* the split second you put your foot down! Top gas economy, smoother idling and low-speed operation . . . faster warm-up, too! And you can get it . . . with horsepower ranging up to 283 . . . on *any* of Chevrolet's 20 models!

That's the big scoop this season — for Chevrolet has more goodies under that bold hood than you'll find this side of Stuttgart! Read this:

FIVE SILK-SMOOTH ENGINES! Four hyper-efficient V8's,* ranging up to 283-cubic-inch displacement and 10.5 to 1 compression ratio. Plus the world's most successful Six, the 140-h.p. "Blue-Flame"!

<u>TWO</u> AUTOMATIC DRIVES!* Velvety Powerglide, of course . . . and now Turboglide, a torque converter with Triple-Turbine take-off and a Hill Retarder for greatly increased "slowing power" on grades!

BOLD "BIG CAR" STYLING! From unified bumper and grille styling back to the dramatic flare of its fender fins, Chevy has the boldest, biggest look in the low-price field! Everything is new, from the Command Post instrument cluster down to its 14-inch wheels. *This* is the car that's giving the competition sleepless nights—and you'll know why when you try it yourself . . . soon!
*Optional at extra cost.

What's under Chevy hoods this year?

FIVE ENGINES!

Nobody else in Chevrolet's field offers such a broad range of performance in so many engine choices. You can have the power you want—just the way you want it in Chevy for '57!

Whatever you want in the way of power, Chevy's got it—but *good!* Want rock-bottom thrift and sturdiness? What could suit you better than the 140-h.p. "Blue-Flame" Six, the world's best tested engine? V8 smoothness with maximum economy? That's the "Turbo-Fire 265" with two-barrel carburetor and 162 h.p.

Like more bottom-end torque and solid *go* all along the line? Try one of Chevy's extra-cost power options. For example, there's the "Turbo-Fire 283" with twin-throat carburetors, 283 cubic inches of displacement, and 185 horses. Then we get into the real scat class—the "Super Turbo-Fire 283" with single four-barrel carburetor, dual exhausts and 220 h.p. Top performer of 'em all is the white-hot Corvette version—up to 283 h.p., 10.5 compression and *fuel injection!* Try 'em on for size at your Chevy dealer's . . . you can't miss! . . . Chevrolet Division of General Motors, Detroit 2, Michigan.

CHEVROLET

1 USA '57 CHEVROLET

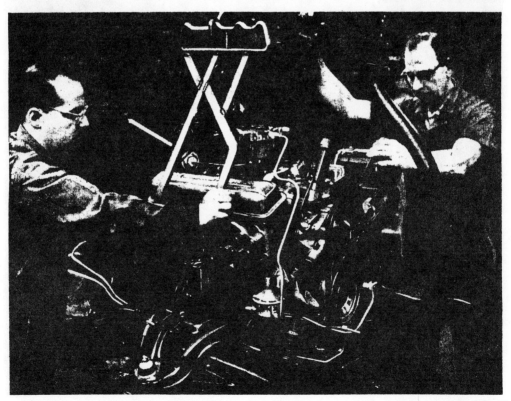

MOTOR TREND/APRIL 1957 **13**

36

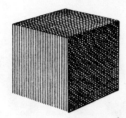

Chevy attains the engineer's dream...

1 H.P. PER CUBIC INCH

Every competitive field has certain magic milestones. In track, the four-minute mile. In aviation, the sound barrier. In mountain climbing, the ascent of Everest . . . and so on.

In American automobile engineering, the magic milestone is this: *one horsepower from every cubic inch of engine displacement!* Chevrolet is the first American production car to achieve this goal; from our 283-cubic-inch V8, with fuel injection* and 10.5 to 1 compression ratio, we pull 283 h.p. Naturally, we're proud. Because this is proof, in cold figures, of the *extra* efficiency of Chevrolet's advanced valve gear, free-breathing manifolding and ultra-short stroke. Better still, it is the warranty of superior engineering in every phase of the car's performance—road-holding, suspension, steering, braking and economy. The real reasons why you get more to be proud of in a Chevrolet—always! . . . *Chevrolet Division of General Motors, Detroit 2, Michigan.*

*Optional at extra cost

Chevy lifts the curtain on tomorrow with—

FUEL INJECTION!

Ramjet fuel injection, optional at extra cost on any Chevrolet model, offers constant-flow port injection.

And that's the beginning of a whole new era of efficiency! For Chevrolet fuel injection puts on the road—today—the precision gas-metering, the instantaneous acceleration that used to be reserved for super-priced custom sports cars. You'll want to take a good long look at this brilliant piece of engineering. But, better still, you'll want to get behind the wheel of a Chevrolet V8 with Ramjet fuel injection—believe us, that's an *experience!* . . . Chevrolet Division of General Motors, Detroit 2, Mich.

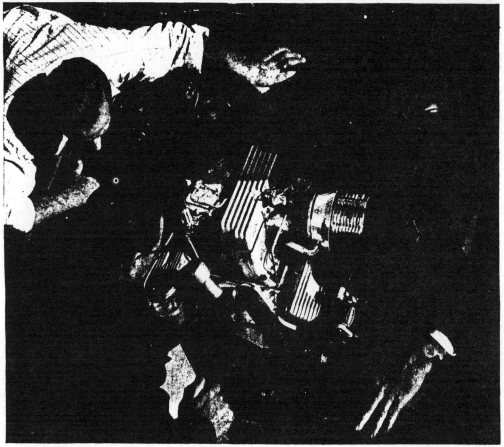

MOTOR TREND/JULY 1957 **13**

Although industry sales slipped due to the recession, Chevrolet managed to produce 1.2 million units and secure a fraction under 30% of the auto market in sales.

"New" is a word much overused in Detroit but this year's Chevy offerings were as new as you can get. From the new "X" frame to the new height, wheelbase and length, to the sheet metal and appointments, these new Chevys made a spectacular splash on the American scene. Also "new" for 1958 was an additional subseries of the Bel Air: the Impala—in Sport Coupe and Convertible form. The Impala was an instant hit with the American public. Also impressive was the amount of chrome trim unique to the Impala. Nonfunctional air intakes were located just behind the doors. Chrome lower body molding ran between the wheelwells. On the Sport Coupe an additional nonfunctional air intake was located on the rear of the roof. The Impala also had a triple taillight arrangement which was unique to it.

While the Impala was the big news this year, there were other major shifts in Chevy's product alignment. The old "One-Fifty" and "Two-Ten" series were replaced by the Delray and Biscayne. "Station Wagons" were also a series on their own. There were a total of 16 models in the four series.

The new models were on a 117.5" wheelbase, length was increased to 209.1", and width increased to 77.7". With everything else all new it was not surprising that an all-new engine was introduced in 1958. This was the 348 cu. in. V-8 generating 250-hp with 2-bbl and 9.5:1 compression or 280-hp with triple 4-bbls and 9.5:1 compression. This was an engine that Chevy had designed with an idea to making it available for both trucks and cars. Despite having more cubic inches, this engine was roundly criticized for being a slug compared to the 283. This was largely due to the 348's extra 1.5" length and extra 2.6" width which made it about 110 lbs. heavier than the 283.

In mid-year Chevy made significant strides in making the 348 a performance engine in keeping with Chevy's hard won reputation as the performance leader. Called the "Law Enforce-ment" engine it turned the 348 into a 315-hp hummer by adding a Duntov cam with solid lifters, heavy-duty clutch and the Corvette close-ratio, 3-speed transmission to the triple 2-bbl carbs. Also included in the package were heavy-duty main and connecting rod bearings plus 11:1 compression. With a 4.56 rear axle, this engine recorded zero to 60 mph time of 7.2 seconds and with a 3.36 rear axle could cruise at 135 mph. No mere 283 would be kicking sand in the 348's face with this set up!

Chevrolet discontinued issuing separate model production figures this year so reliable estimates are hard to come by. By body type totals were: 4d Sdn, 491,441; 2d Sdn, 256,182; 4d Wgn, 170,473; Spts Cpe, 142,592; Spts Sdn, 83,330; Convertible, 55,989; 2d Wgn, 16,590. It has been estimated by other authors that series production was: Delray, 178,000; Biscayne, 377,000; Bel Air, 532,000; and Station Wagons, 187,000. The series estimates differ marginally from the body type totals issued by Chevrolet. Impala Convertible production has been estimated at 55,989 by one author and 60,000 by another. No independent verification from Chevrolet is available.

The least expensive Chevrolet (passenger car) was the two-door sedan at $2,208 (3,399 lbs.) and the most expensive was the Bel Air Impala Convertible at $2,841 (3,523 lbs.). The two-door Biscayne sedan was $2,343 (3,407 lbs.) and the two-door Bel Air sedan was $2,493 (3,427 lbs.).

Literature issued this year consisted of the full-line Chevrolet brochure (pages 40-43) and a full-line folder. Chevrolet ads no longer placed much stress on high performance (page 44).

THE IMPALA SPORT COUPE
IN SILVER BLUE AND SNOWCREST WHITE

Newest heartthrob in sight—the Impala Sport Coupe. *Longer* by over
nine inches, *lower* by more than two, the Impala, like every '58 Chevy,
wears the look of a car just naturally born for the road. Begin at its
massive new grille and dual roadlights . . . sweep your glance
along its taut, sleek length. This is the *newest*—that's for sure!

SPECIFICATIONS

STATION WAGON AND CORVETTE SPECIFICATIONS IN SEPARATE CATALOGS

CHOOSE FROM 18 POWER TEAMS —AVAILABLE IN EVERY MODEL—

See your Chevrolet dealer for prices

	Turboglide	Powerglide	Overdrive	Synchro-Mesh
280-h.p. Super Turbo-Thrust V8 348 cu. in., 9.5:1 compr. ratio Triple two-barrel carburetion	●	●		●
250-h.p. Turbo-Thrust V8 348 cu. in., 9.5:1 compr. ratio Four-barrel carburetion	●	●		●
250-h.p. Ramjet Fuel Injection V8 283 cu. in., 9.5:1 compr. ratio Ramjet Fuel Injection		●	●	●
230-h.p. Super Turbo-Fire V8 283 cu. in., 9.5:1 compr. ratio Four-barrel carburetion	●	●	●	●
185-h.p. Turbo-Fire V8 283 cu. in., 8.5:1 compr. ratio Two-barrel carburetion	●	●	●	●
145-h.p. Blue-Flame 6 235.5 cu. in., 8.25:1 compr. ratio Single-barrel carburetion	●	●	●	●

ENGINE

All Chevrolet engines feature valve-in-head design, hydraulic valve lifters, aluminum pistons, forged steel crankshaft, replaceable-insert main and connecting rod bearings, full-pressure lubrication, harmonic balancer, 12-volt electrical system, positive-shift starter, automatic choke, 3-point mounting. V8 engines feature independent operating mechanism for each valve, integral valve guides, chain-driven camshaft, five main bearings, full-flow oil filter*, four-quart oil

refill (without filter), and dual exhaust system (optional* on Turbo-Fire V8 and Super Turbo-Thrust V8 engines). Turbo-Thrust V8 and Super Turbo-Thrust V8 engines have precision machined-in-bore combustion chambers and large free-flow valves. Blue-Flame 6 engine has shaft-mounted rocker arms, replaceable valve guides, four main bearings, gear-driven camshaft, by-pass type oil filter*, five-quart oil refill (without filter).

TRANSMISSION

TURBOGLIDE*—Five-element torque converter with pump, three turbines, and dual-pitch stator controlled by accelerator pedal, two turbine-operated planetary gear sets. Single forward "Drive" range, Grade retarder, powerful reverse, and positive parking lock. Selector sequence P-R-N-D-GR.

POWERGLIDE*—Three-element torque converter (pump, turbine and stator) with automatically controlled planetary gears in "Drive" range, manually selected for "Low", and "reverse." Positive parking lock. Selector sequence P-R-N-D-L.

OVERDRIVE*—3-speed Synchro-Mesh plus 2-speed planetary overdrive, engaged semi-automatically above approximately 30 m.p.h. Downshift to direct drive by flooring accelerator. Lock-out control handle.

SYNCHRO-MESH—3-speed all helical gear Synchro-Mesh with high torque capacity. Gear ratios matched to power team: 348-cu.-in. V8 first 2.21:1, second 1.32:1, third 1:1, reverse 2.51:1; 283-cu.-in. V8 first 2.47:1, second 1.53:1, third 1:1, reverse 2.80:1; 6-cyl. first and reverse 2.94:1, second 1.68:1, third 1:1.

CLUTCH

9½-inch diaphragm spring type with Blue-Flame 6 engine. 10-inch semi-centrifugal diaphragm spring type with Turbo-Fire V8, Super Turbo-Fire V8 and Ramjet Fuel Injection V8 engines. 10½-inch semi-centrifugal coil spring type with Turbo-Thrust V8 and Super Turbo-Thrust V8 engines. All clutches have cushioned disc and permanently lubricated throw-out bearing.

CHASSIS

SAFETY-GIRDER FRAME—Low, rigid tunnel-center X-built. **FULL COIL SUSPENSION**—Four coil springs with double-acting shock absorbers and built-in leveling control. Independent front suspension with spherical joints, four-link rear suspension with rugged control arms above and below axle. Ride stabilizer bar on V8 models. **WHEELS AND TIRES**—14" wheels, 7.50 x 14 4-ply rating on V8 models; tubeless tires, 8.00 x 14 4-ply rating on convertible). **BRAKES**—Hydraulic, self-energizing 11" Jumbo-Drum with Bonded linings. Foot-operated mechanical parking brakes, fingertip release. **STEERING**—Forward-mounted Ball-Race gear, balanced relay linkage. Overall ratio 23:1. **REAR AXLE**—Hypoid, semi-floating, ratio matched to power team. **FUEL TANK**—20-gallon capacity. **ELECTRICAL**—12-volt system, 54-plate battery, 30-ampere generator.

BODY

STRUCTURE—All-welded Fisher Unisteel construction, sealed and insulated, 12-point mounting. **EXTERIOR**—Polished lacquer finish, distinctive trim and identification for each series, horizontal dual headlights, directional signals, high-level cowl air intake, concealed fuel filler. **APPOINTMENTS**—Single key locks, push-button door handles, crank-operated front vent windows, 2-speed electric windshield wipers (vacuum-boosted type with Blue-Flame 6 engine). **INTERIOR**—Luxurious combinations of nylon-faced fabric and vinyl seats (all-vinyl in convertible). Vinyl side trim. Two-spoke 17" recessed-hub steering wheel, and instrument panel distinctive for each series. Enclosed steering column.

DIMENSIONS

Wheelbase, 117.5'. Front and rear tread, 58.8". Overall length 209.1", width 77.7", height Impala Sport Coupe 56.4", Impala Convertible 56.5", other models 57.4".

OPTIONAL EQUIPMENT*

Power steering, Power brakes, Power window**, Power front seats**, Heavy-duty rear coil springs, Level-Air suspension**, Positraction rear axle, Heavy-duty clutch**, E-Z-Eye glass, Padded instrument panel, Heater and defroster, Air conditioners**, White-wall and 8.00 x 14 4-ply black tires, Choice of radios, Oil filter, Heavy-duty generator**, Heavy-duty battery**, Oil-bath air cleaner, positive crankcase ventilation system**, engine governor**, and electric windshield wiper for Blue-Flame 6 engine. Full line of accessory equipment.

POWER ASSISTS*

Touch a button here, press a pedal there—like magic new driving fun is yours in the '58 Chevy!

POWER STEERING lets you enjoy fingertip ease and safety with its effortless parking, in full-time control.

POWER BRAKES add to your assurance by yielding over a ton of stopping force at the touch of a toe.

ALL-WEATHER AIR CONDITIONING makes your car a haven of comfort—puts "fair weather" at your automatic bidding.

POWER SEAT—POWER WINDOWS meet your personal demands for individual comfort . . . it's all done with quiet electrical power.

*Optional at extra cost. **Availability determined by either model or equipment.

ALL ILLUSTRATIONS AND SPECIFICATIONS CONTAINED IN THIS LITERATURE ARE BASED ON THE LATEST PRODUCT INFORMATION AVAILABLE AT THE TIME OF PUBLICATION APPROVAL. THE RIGHT IS RESERVED TO MAKE CHANGES AT ANY TIME WITHOUT NOTICE IN PRICES, COLORS, MATERIALS, EQUIPMENT, SPECIFICATIONS AND MODELS, AND ALSO TO DISCONTINUE MODELS.

CHEVROLET MOTOR DIVISION • GENERAL MOTORS CORPORATION, DETROIT 2, MICHIGAN

NO CAR IN CHEVROLET'S FIELD BRINGS YOU MORE DEEP-DOWN NEWNESS . . . WITH BIG NEW CHANGES FROM ROAD TO ROOF!

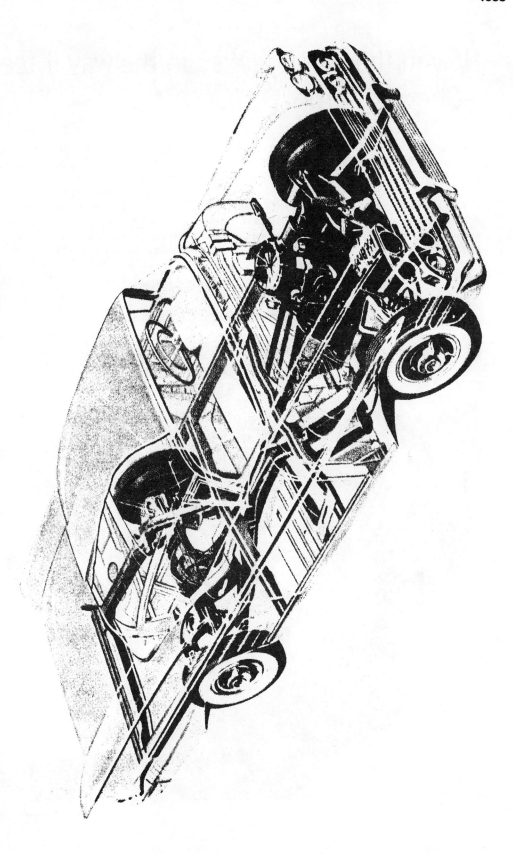

New in the way it looks...in the way it feels —Chevy's Turbo-Thrust V8!

Here's an engineering achievement you can feel the instant your toe touches the treadle. You feel a new kind of response—an ultra-smooth pickup. And when you lift that Chevrolet hood you'll see why. You'll see an engine so radical it even <u>looks</u> different. It's the Turbo-Thrust V8. It's built around a revolutionary design that contributes to constant smoothness at <u>all</u> engine speeds and to exceptional efficiency as well.

Turbo-Thrust's combustion chambers are located in the cylinder block rather than in the cylinder head. They're wedge-shaped and precision machined

for even, efficient combustion. Since each chamber is precisely the same size, each piston does the same work. The result is a velvet-smooth flow of power from idling speed right on up. A whopping 348 cubic inches of displacement gives you power when you need it—with plenty in reserve. Visit your Chevrolet dealer today. Lift the hood and see the difference . . . take a drive and you'll <u>feel</u> it!

The 250-h.p. Turbo-Thrust V8—or the 280-h.p. Super Turbo-Thrust V8—is available at extra cost in any Chevrolet. . . . Chevrolet Division of General Motors, Detroit 2, Michigan.

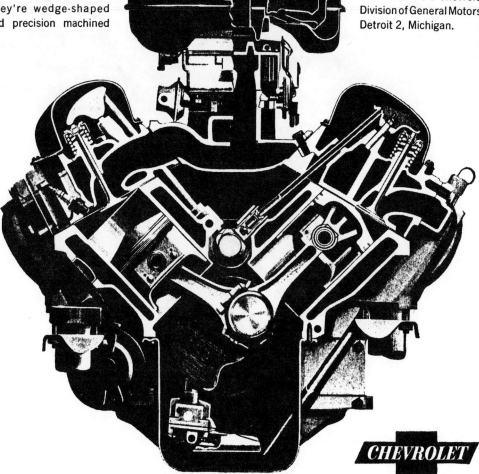

CHEVROLET

Industry sales rebounded from 1958 with Chevrolet calendar year sales up to 1,528,592. This was slightly behind Ford due to a six week steel strike in late 1959 which hurt Chevrolet production.

This, of course, was the year that the fin was in. Although normally one would not expect a radically new car a year after an all-new car had been introduced, it would happen this year. This was because a corporate GM edict that key structural elements would be shared between divisions just chanced to take effect this year.

In addition to the radically new Chevys, there was also a reshuffling of the series designations. The Delray was gone and the Biscayne became the economy series, the Bel Air was relegated to middle-range series. The Impala became a series of its own with two new models (a four-door hardtop and sedan) and was then the premier Chevrolet offering. The Nomad wagon was now based on the Impala.

The Impala was distinguished from the rest of the series by the Impala identifier inset on the side chrome trim and the chrome tail carried from the hood ornaments back to the windshield. Vertical chrome strips divided the cat's-eye taillights, center of the rear deck lid and nonfunctional air scoops faced the rear from the roof rear. Crossed flags above the hood ornament also identified the Impala.

Impala interiors continued to feature front and rear arm rests and a higher grade of carpeting, fabric and vinyl. A sporty steering wheel helped maintain the interior distinction of the Impala.

The wheelbase was increased this year to 119", where it would remain through the musclecar era, and end with the 1970 models. Overall length increased to 210.9" and width to 79.9" while height decreased to 54" (except for sedans at 56" and wagons at 56.3").

Engine availability was the same 283 and 348 V-8 line-up as in 1958. Horsepower, however, was up on the 348 to a maximum of 335-hp with a triple 2-bbl carb setup and 11.25:1 compression (one author suggests the maximum horsepower rating was 345 with this setup but 335-hp is the maximum listed by Chevrolet.)

Production by body style (including Corvette) was as follows: 4d Sdn, 525,461; 2d Sdn, 281,924; 4d Wgn, 188,623; Spts Sdn, 182,520; Spts Cpe, 164,901; Convert, 72,765; 2d Wgn, 20,760. Estimates of production by series do not completely reconcile with the official totals but are worth mentioning as being reliable approximations: Biscayne, 311,800; Bel Air, 447,100; Impala, 473,000 (including an estimated 65,800 Convertibles); Wagons, 239,400.

The least expensive Chevrolet (passenger car excluding station wagons) was the Biscayne two-door sedan with a base price of $2,365 (3,530 lbs.) and the most expensive was the Impala Convertible at $2,967 (3,650 lbs.). The Bel Air two-door sedan had a base price of $2,504 (3,510 lbs.). The four-door Impala sedan $2,710 (3,620 lbs.).

Literature this year was limited. The full-line Chevrolet catalogue (pages 46-52) and a folder with the same cover were the main pieces.

CHEVROLET '59

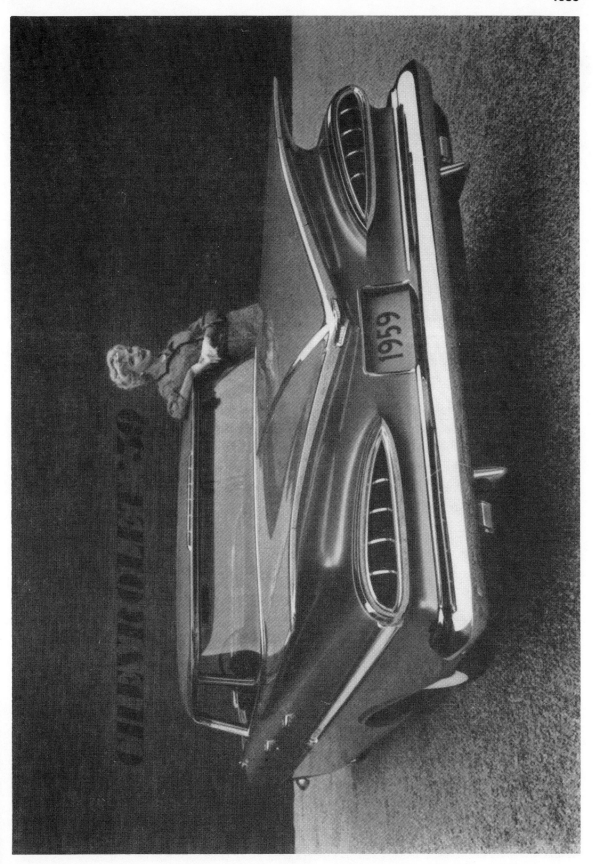

Functional horsepower—the logical design approach to driving pleasure. Not for speed's sake alone, but for safe, dependable going—in all kinds of weather, in city traffic or on the road. *Thrifty* going, too—with Chevrolet's standard 6 and V8, both offering the economy of *regular* fuel. The valve-in-head leader makes it all yours in the industry's most advanced power teams for '59!

250-HP Turbo-Thrust V8*—In an engine cubic inches are muscles— and here are 348 of them ready to do your instant bidding with a reserve of smooth, quiet *functional* power for any situation. Featured are 4-barrel carburetion, new high efficiency air cleaner, full dual exhaust system, hydraulic valve lifters and high 9.5 to 1 compression ratio.

280-HP Super Turbo-Thrust V8*—Triple two-barrel carburetors offer single-carburetor economy for normal driving, coupled with a full-power boost when you need it.

250-HP Ramjet Fuel Injection V8*—Instant throttle response from idle to cruising speed, with ordinary carburetors eliminated. Fast cold weather starts, high over-all fuel economy: all features of Ramjet Fuel Injection—greatest engine advance since overhead valves.

185-HP Turbo-Fire V8—Standard V8 in all series, combines the savings of *regular* fuel with the smoothness of V8 design; 283-cu.-in. displacement and single two-barrel carburetor. Its compact, lightweight short-stroke design promotes long life and quiet operation. Top features: hydraulic valve lifters, new high-efficiency dry air cleaner, new integral fuel filter. Single exhaust standard; dual exhaust extra-cost option.

230-HP Super Turbo-Fire V8*—Here's big engine performance at low cost with the same advanced design of its 283-cu.-in. running mate, plus a performance bonus of extra-high 9.5 to 1 compression ratio and efficient 4-barrel carburetion. Dual exhaust system with resonators is available as an extra-cost option.

now—up to 10% fuel savings with new Hi-Thrift 6!

The valve-in-head leader has done it again—bringing you new economy with the introduction for '59 of a new fuel-thrifty 6 that gets extra miles from every tankful. You'll enjoy spirited performance from regular grades of fuel—and more usable power at everyday driving speeds.

*Extra-cost option

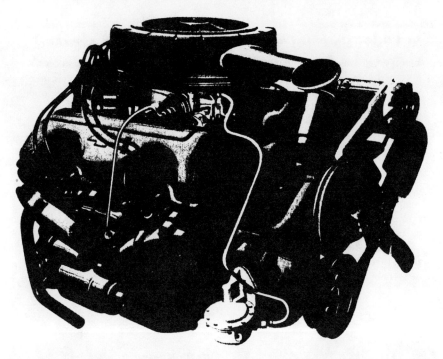

TURBO-THRUST V8—Instant response and high compression

HI-THRIFT 6—Adding extra miles to every tank of fuel

in CHASSIS, too, Chevy's newness goes down deep!

You'll enjoy easier, surer handling and a softer, steadier ride in this vastly improved chassis for '59. There's a new solid road-feel, thanks to Chevy's increased wheelbase and the super rigidity of its X-built Safety-Girder frame. You'll guide the car with less effort with the crisp control of Ball-Race steering. A new lateral control bar steadies the rear suspension for greater smoothness; there's a notable absence of rear-end squat and lift.

every tire on every '59 Chevrolet has all-new Tyrex!

All-new Tyrex—super-tough tire cord that puts tire design years ahead— is standard equipment on your '59 Chevy. Possessing remarkable strength and resiliency, Tyrex offers greater blowout protection, added safety, extra miles of wear. Tyrex cord makes tires lighter, more flexible—lets them roll *easier*, contributing to better fuel mileage, and *softer* for a better ride. And for extra smoothness from your very first mile, wheels and tires (even spare) are pre-balanced in assembly, a *first* in Chevrolet's field!

New Safety-Master brakes—In the '59 Chevy braking is surer—27% more bonded lining area sees safely to that! Chevy's new air-cooled giant sized brakes are up to 66% more durable, too. New wider drums are cooled in an air-stream to keep brake temperatures *down* and stopping force *up*. Even Chevy's new wheels are designed to act as brake-cooling fans!

Luxurious Level Air suspension*—As great a ride as ever offered on any car! Not until you've experienced its *super-softness* will you fully know how floating-smooth travel can really be. For '59, new air ride design means extra durability, quietness and long, trouble-free life!

*Extra-cost option

Standard Full Coil suspension—Even greater in '59! Flexible coils at each wheel give full-time cushioning on roughest roads. Unlike ordinary leaf springs, independent coils are isolated from driving and braking forces, free for the job of smoothing your ride.

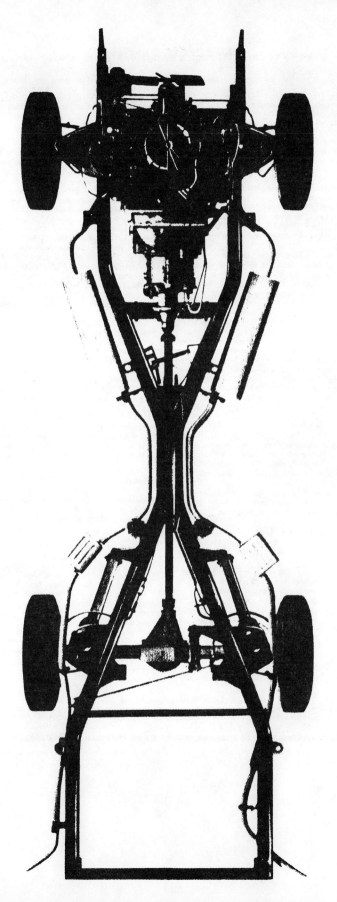

specifications

engine

135-H.P. HI-THRIFT 6: 235.5 cu. in., 8.25:1 compression ratio, single-barrel carburetion, single exhaust. 185-H.P. TURBO-FIRE V8: 283 cu. in., 8.5:1 compression ratio, two-barrel carburetion, single exhaust (dual optional*). 230-H.P. SUPER TURBO-FIRE V8*: 283 cu. in., 9.5:1 compression ratio, four-barrel carburetion, single exhaust (dual optional*). 250-H.P. RAMJET FUEL INJECTION V8*: 283 cu. in., 9.5:1 compression ratio, Ramjet Fuel Injection, dual exhaust. 250-H.P. TURBO-THRUST V8*: 348 cu. in., 9.5:1 compression ratio, four-barrel carburetion, dual exhaust. 280-H.P. SUPER TURBO-THRUST V8*: 348 cu. in., 9.5:1 compression ratio, triple two-barrel carburetion, dual exhaust. 290-H.P. RAMJET SPECIAL V8*: 283 cu. in., 10.5:1 compression ratio, Ramjet Fuel Injection, dual exhaust. 320-H.P. TURBO-THRUST SPECIAL V8*: 348 cu. in., 11.25:1 compression ratio, four-barrel carburetion, dual exhaust (305 H.P., 11:1 compression ratio with Powerglide). 335-H.P., SUPER TURBO-THRUST SPECIAL V8*: 348 cu. in., 11.25:1 compression ratio, triple two-barrel carburetion, dual exhaust.

All Chevrolet engines feature valve-in-head design, aluminum pistons, forged steel crankshaft, replaceable-insert main and connecting rod bearings, full-pressure lubrication, harmonic balancer, 12-volt electrical system, positive-shift starter, automatic choke, 3-point mounting. Hydraulic valve lifters standard on all except special V8 engines. V8 engines feature independent operating mechanism for each valve, integral valve guides, chain-driven camshaft, five main bearings, paper element type air cleaner, full-flow oil filter* (standard with fuel injection, mandatory with special 348-cu.-in. engines), four-quart oil refill (without filter), and dual exhaust system with resonators (optional* on Turbo-Fire V8 and Super Turbo-Fire V8). Turbo-Thrust V8 and Super Turbo-Thrust V8 have precision machined-in-bore combustion chambers and large free-flow valves. Hi-Thrift 6 engine has shaft-mounted rocker arms, replaceable valve guides, four main bearings, gear-driven camshaft, oil-wetted air cleaner, by-pass type oil filter*, five-quart oil refill (without filter). Special V8 engines include special camshaft and valve system with mechanical valve lifters, premium bearings, and other heavy-duty features.

transmission

TURBOGLIDE*—Five-element torque converter with pump, three turbines, and dual-pitch stator controlled by accelerator pedal. Two turbine-operated planetary gear sets. Single forward Drive range. Grade Retarder, powerful reverse, and positive parking lock. Selector sequence P-R-N-D-Gr.

POWERGLIDE*—Three-element torque converter (pump, turbine and stator) with automatically controlled planetary gears in Drive range, manually selected for low and reverse. Positive parking lock. Selector sequence P-R-N-D-L.

4-SPEED SYNCHRO-MESH*—Close-ratio 4-Speed Synchro-Mesh design, all forward speeds fully synchronized. Central floor-mounted short-stroke shift lever. Gear ratios: First 2.20:1, second 1.66:1, third 1.31:1, fourth 1:1, reverse 2.26:1.

OVERDRIVE*—3-Speed Synchro-Mesh plus 2-speed planetary overdrive, engaged semi-automatically above approximately 30 m.p.h. Downshift to direct drive by flooring accelerator. Lock-out control handle.

3-SPEED SYNCHRO-MESH—All helical gear Synchro-Mesh design with high torque capacity. Gear ratios matched to power team: V8 first 2.47:1, second 1.53:1, third 1:1, reverse 2.80:1; all Overdrive and with 6-cylinder engines first and reverse 2.94:1, second 1.68:1, third 1:1.

clutch

9½-inch diaphragm spring type with Hi-Thrift 6 engine. 10-inch semi-centrifugal diaphragm spring type with Turbo-Fire V8, Super Turbo-Fire V8 and Ramjet Fuel Injection V8 engines. 10½-inch semi-centrifugal diaphragm spring type with Turbo-Thrust V8 and Super Turbo-Thrust V8 engines. All clutches have cushioned disc and permanently lubricated throw-out bearing.

chassis

SAFETY-GIRDER FRAME—Low, rigid tunnel-center X-built. FULL COIL SUSPENSION—Four coil springs with double-acting shock absorbers and built-in levelizing control, front and rear. Independent front suspension with spherical joints, ride stabilizer bar on all except 6-cylinder Bel Air and Biscayne models. Four-link rear suspension with four rugged rubber-bushed control arms. WHEELS AND TIRES—14" wheels, 7.50 x 14 4-ply rating low-pressure blackwall tubeless tires (8.00 x 14 4-ply rating on Convertible and Station Wagons). BRAKES—Hydraulic, self-energizing 11" Safety-Master brakes with bonded linings, area 199.5 square inches. Foot-operated mechanical parking brakes, finger-tip release. STEERING—Forward-mounted Ball-Race gear, balanced relay linkage. Overall ratio 28:1 standard, 24:1 with power steering*. REAR AXLE—Hypoid, semi-floating, four ratios tailored to power teams. FUEL CAPACITY—Station Wagons, 17 gals. (Kingswood, 18 gals.), all others, 20 gals. ELECTRICAL—12-volt system, 54-plate battery (66-plate with special 348-cu.-in. V8 engines), 30-ampere generator.

body

STRUCTURE—All-welded Fisher Unisteel construction, sealed and insulated, 12-point mounting. EXTERIOR—Magic-Mirror acrylic lacquer finish, distinctive trim and identification for each series, horizontal dual headlights, directional signals, high-level air intake, concealed fuel filler. Safety *Plate* Glass in all windows. APPOINTMENTS—Single key locks, push-button door handles, crank-operated front vent windows, electric windshield wipers. INTERIOR—Luxurious combinations of nylon-faced fabric and vinyl upholstery (all vinyl in Convertible and Brookwood Station Wagons). Vinyl side trim and headlining (cloth headlining in Impala 4-door sedan, Bel Air and Biscayne models). 2-spoke 17" recessed-hub steering wheel and instrument panel distinctive for each series. Enclosed steering column.

dimensions

Wheelbase, 119". Front and rear tread, 60.3" and 59.3". Overall: length 210.9", width 79.9", height—Sport Sedan, Sport Coupe and Convertible 54.0", Sedans 56.0", Station Wagons 56.3".

*optional equipment**

Power steering. Power brakes. Power windows**. Flexomatic 6-Way power front seat**. Power tailgate window**. Vented full wheel covers. Heavy-duty rear coil springs. Positraction rear axle. Heavy-duty clutch**. E-Z-Eye glass. Padded instrument panel. De luxe equipment, steering wheel and foam rubber front seat cushion for Biscayne and Brookwood models. Heater and defroster. Air conditioner**. Whitewall and 8.00 x 14 4-ply tires. Choice of radios. Dual exhaust**. Oil filter. Heavy-duty generator**. Heavy-duty battery. Two-speed electric windshield wiper and pushbutton windshield washer. Oil-bath air cleaner for Hi-Thrift 6 engine. Special equipment for police or taxicab service. Full line of accessory equipment.

*Optional at extra cost. **Availability determined by either model or equipment.

Chevrolet Motor Division • *General Motors Corporation, Detroit 2, Michigan*

This was generally a year of good industry sales and Chevrolet shared in the increase. After two years of radical change, Chevrolet was satisfied with relatively minor changes to its basic models. The major news this year was the introduction of the revolutionary Corvair.

It is generally agreed that the 1960 facelift of the Chevy line was a good one. The exaggerated finning was toned down and the handsome new grille subdued the aggressive appearance of the 1959 models.

The Impala continued as a series with four models: Sport Sedan, Sport Coupe, 4-door Sedan and Convertible. The Impala was distinguished from the Bel Air series by a more dressy appearance caused largely by the increased amount of chrome trim and details like the nonfunctional air intake scoops located in the lower rear window molding (eliminated on the convertible). Replacing the cat's-eyes of 1959 was a triple taillight arrangement distinctly reminiscent of 1958. Also on the Impala, four parallel bar moldings were split by the chromed, short side molding which extended from the front lights to the wheel well. A filled area with the Impala script and crossed flags extended from the rocket emblem back to the taillights. The rear body panel consisted of thin, vertical, blacked-out areas as opposed to the

Bel Air's rather Plain Jane look. The Nomad station wagon continued to be based on the Impala.

Overall length was decreased infintessimally by standard V-8 powerplant remained the 170-hp 283 cu. in. V-8 available with Powerglide transmission, 3-speed synchromesh and Overdrive. The maximum output engine was named the "Super Turbo-Thrust Special V8" and was rated at 335-hp with triple 2-bbl carbs, dual exhaust and 11.25:1 compression.

Again, Chevrolet did not release production figures by series. Production was: 4d Sdn, 497,048; 2d Sdn, 228,322; Spts Cpe, 204,467; 4d Wgn, 198,066; Spts Sdn, 169,016; Convtble, 79,903; 2d Wgn, 14,663. Series production has been estimated to have been: Biscayne, 287,662; Bel Air, 381,517; Impala, 511,925 (including 100,000 convertibles); Station Wagons, 212,729.

The least expensive Chevrolet (passenger car excluding station wagons) was the two-door Biscayne sedan with a base price of $2,369 (3,500 lbs.) and the most expensive was the Impala Convertible at $2,954 (3,635 lbs.). The two-door Bel Air sedan was $2,491 (3,505 lbs.). The four-door Impala sedan was $2,697 (3,580 lbs.).

Literature this year included the full-line Chevrolet catalogue (pages 54-58) and a saver folder.

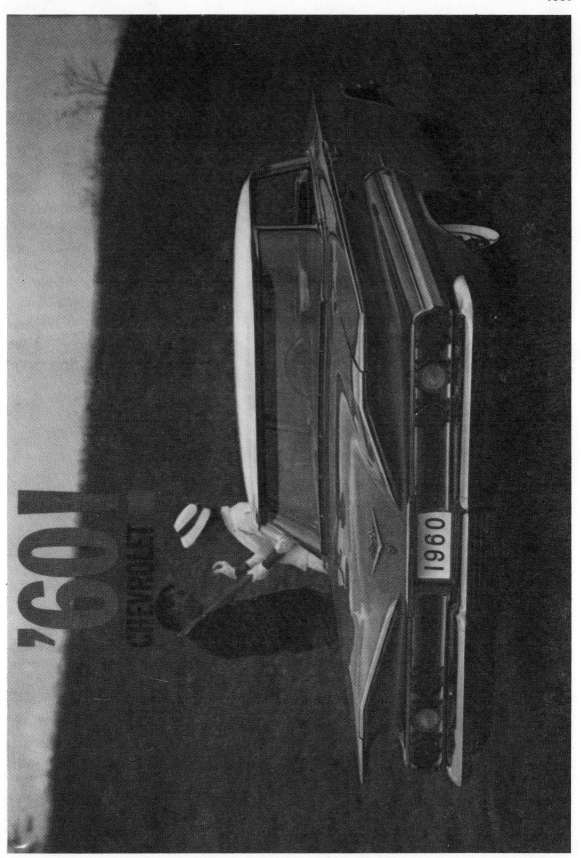

GREAT NEW LINEUP OF FAMOUS CHEVROLET V8's FOR 1960!

V8 GAS SAVINGS. Chevrolet takes the lead in V8 economy with the introduction of the new standard 283-cu.-in. economy TURBO-FIRE V8, designed to deliver top economy along with spirited performance. A new economy-contoured camshaft gives cleaner, more efficient fuel burning plus more torque in the low and middle speed ranges you use most. The result: fuel savings are exceptional and you use regular gas. Specially calibrated, high-efficiency two-barrel carburetor contributes further to fuel economy. In addition, reduced axle ratio is a money-saving feature. A newly designed cylinder head saves on oil. In addition, full-flow oil filter is standard on this and every Chevrolet V8 engine. Dual exhaust system is optional at extra cost. Compression ratio 8.5 to 1; 170 h.p.

PERFORMANCE WITH A PURPOSE. Four-barrel carburetion in the husky 283-cu.-in. SUPER TURBO-FIRE V8* gives you that extra surge of power you need for any occasion. At moderate speeds you get thrifty two-barrel operation automatically. New cylinder head design helps you save on oil. Dual exhaust system is optional at extra cost. Compression ratio: 9.5 to 1; 230 h.p.

DEEP-CHESTED STAMINA. Here's a big engine with special smoothness, quietness and efficiency. The wedge-shaped combustion chambers of Chevrolet's big-displacement 348-cu.-in. TURBO-THRUST V8* are precision-machined for better use of fuel, finer performance, smooth, quiet power from every gallon of fuel. Four-barrel carburetion, high-efficiency air cleaner and dual exhaust system are standard. Compression ratio 9.5 to 1; 250 h.p.

POWER FOR ANY NEED. Triple two-barrel carburetion provides the power boost in the Chevrolet 348-cu.-in. SUPER TURBO-THRUST V8*. When you need it, 280 h.p. is at your command. At regular driving speeds, the SUPER TURBO-THRUST V8 performs economically with two-barrel carburetion. Dual exhaust system is standard. Compression ratio: 9.5 to 1. *Optional at extra cost.

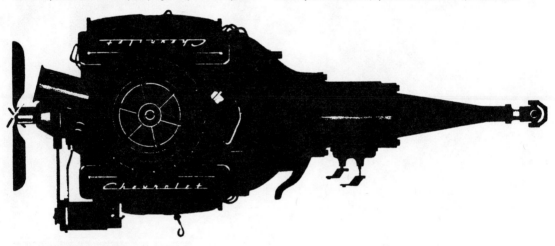

BIG SAVINGS WITH CHEVY'S 6!

Chevrolet's HI-THRIFT 6 is a real economy leader among full-sized car engines. Yet this advanced 6, standard equipment in any Chevy, performs with the spirit and quietness of a V8. Here are just a few reasons why HI-THRIFT is the industry's most popular 6: quiet-operating hydraulic valve lifters give smoother performance . . . cut maintenance costs because valves never need adjustment. Standard automatic choke saves fuel by giving you just the right mixture for smooth, economical warm-up. Compression ratio 8.25 to 1; 000 h.p.

SELECT FROM THE INDUSTRY'S WIDEST CHOICE OF POWER TEAMS

	Turboglide	Powerglide	4-Speed Synchro-Mesh	3-Speed Synchro-Mesh	Overdrive
280-h.p. Super Turbo-Thrust V8**	X	X	X	X	
250-h.p. Turbo-Thrust V8**.......	X	X	X	X	
230-h.p. Super Turbo-Fire V8.....	X	X		X	X
170-h.p. Turbo-Fire V8...........	X	X		X	X
135-h.p. Hi-Thrift 6.............		X		X	X

**These two engines, modified for special uses, are available with power ratings of 335 h.p. and 320 h.p., respectively, with either 3-Speed or 4-Speed Synchro-Mesh transmissions. Also 305 h.p. available with heavy-duty Powerglide.

SPIRITED, ECONOMICAL PERFORMANCE

CHOICE OF FIVE TRANSMISSIONS

For real luxury, there's Chevy's TURBOGLIDE*—unsurpassed in automatic driving . . . not even a suggestion of a shift in "Drive" position. Thoroughly tested and engineered for exceptionally durable performance, TURBOGLIDE is the ultimate in driving smoothness and quietness. The most popular automatic transmission in the low-price field is offered by Chevrolet, too. It's POWERGLIDE*—dependable, smooth and responsive.

Chevy's 4-SPEED SYNCHRO-MESH* transmission is the perfect companion for a really spirited engine giving you sports-car-like action. Standard 3-SPEED SYNCHRO-MESH is as effortless and dependable as any manual shifting ever offered. For top economy, choose Chevrolet OVERDRIVE* for fewer engine revolutions with every turn of the wheels. Saves you fuel, plus engine wear.

*Optional at extra cost.

POSITRACTION* REAR AXLE puts the power where it counts. You need traction with only one rear wheel to get out of snow, ice, mud or sand—because Positraction directs most of the power to the wheel that grips.

SPECIFICATIONS**

**For Corvair and Corvette specifications, see separate catalogs.

BODY—All-welded Fisher Unisteel construction, sealed and insulated, acoustically hushed, extra-large rubber mountings. Double-walled cowl, extra-heavy side rails and integral body crossmembers, High-Level air intake. Magic-Mirror acrylic lacquer finish. Safety Plate Glass in all windows. Roll-down rear window in Station Wagons. Single-key locking system, pushbutton door handles. Interiors color-keyed to car exterior, all-vinyl sidewall trim.

BISCAYNE AND BROOKWOOD STANDARD FEATURES—Distinctive trim and identification, dual electric windshield wipers, directional signals, enclosed steering column, 17″ recessed-hub steering wheel with horn button, foam cushioned front seats, armrests on front doors, dual adjustable sun visors, cigarette lighter, glove compartment lock. Nylon-faced pattern cloth seat upholstery in Biscayne—simulated-weave vinyl in Brookwood.

BEL AIR, PARKWOOD, AND KINGSWOOD ADDITIONAL FEATURES—Distinctive trim and identification, foam cushioned rear seats, nylon-faced pattern cloth seat upholstery (woven plastic in Parkwood and Kingswood). Cloth headlining (all vinyl in Parkwood and Kingswood). Horn ring, rear armrests, glove compartment light, automatic front door light switches, combination carpet and vinyl-coated rubber floor mats, plus Biscayne and Brookwood standard equipment. Power-operated rear window on Kingswood.

IMPALA AND NOMAD ADDITIONAL FEATURES—Distinctive trim and identification, electric clock, parking brake warning light. Distinctive pattern nylon-faced seat upholstery (simulated cloth pattern vinyl in Convertible), full-carpet floor mats (combination carpet and vinyl-coated floor mats in Convertible), vinyl headlining (cloth in 4-Door Sedan). Dual backup lights—plus Biscayne Brookwood, Bel Air, and Parkwood standard equipment.

ENGINE—HI-THRIFT 6: 135 h.p., 235.5 cu. in., 8.25:1 compression ratio, single barrel carburetion, single exhaust. TURBO-FIRE V8: 170 h. p., 283 cu. in., 8.5:1 c. r., two-barrel carburetion, single exhaust (dual optional*). SUPER TURBO-FIRE V8*: 230 h.p., 283 cu. in., 9.5:1 c. r., four-barrel carburetion, single exhaust (dual optional*). TURBO-THRUST V8*: 250 h.p., 348 cu. in., 9.5:1 c. r., four-barrel carburetion, dual exhaust. SUPER TURBO-THRUST V8*: 280 h.p. 348 cu. in., 9.5:1 c. r., triple two-barrel carburetion, dual exhaust. TURBO-THRUST SPECIAL V8*: 305 h.p. and 11:1 c. r. with Powerglide, 320 h.p. and 11.25:1 c. r. with 3- or 4-Speed Synchro-Mesh, 348 cu. in., four-barrel carburetion, dual exhaust. SUPER TURBO-THRUST SPECIAL V8*: 335 h.p., 348 cu. in., 11.25:1 c. r., triple two-barrel carburetion, dual exhaust.

1960 Chevrolet engines feature valve-in-head design, aluminum pistons, forged steel crankshaft, positive-shift starter, and automatic choke. Hydraulic valve lifters on all except special V8 engines. Turbo-Fire V8 engine has oil-wetted air cleaner, other V8 engines paper element type. Full-flow oil filter with all V8 engines. Hi-Thrift 6 has oil-wetted air cleaner and by-pass type oil filter*. Special V8 engines include special camshaft and valve system with mechanical valve lifters, and other heavy-duty features.

TRANSMISSION—TURBOGLIDE*: Five-element torque converter with pump, three turbines, and dual-pitch stator. Grade Retarder. Positive parking lock. Selector sequence P-R-N-D-Gr.

POWERGLIDE*: Three-element torque converter with hydraulically controlled planetary gears. Positive parking lock. Selector sequence P-R-N-D-L.

4-SPEED SYNCHRO-MESH*: Close-ratio design, all forward gears fully synchronized. Central floor-mounted shift lever.

OVERDRIVE*: 3-Speed Synchro-Mesh plus 2-speed planetary overdrive, engaged semi-automatically above approximately 30 m.p.h.

3-SPEED SYNCHRO-MESH: All-helical gear design with high torque capacity. Gear ratios matched to power team.

CLUTCH—9½-inch diaphragm spring type with Hi-Thrift 6 engine, 10″ with Turbo-Fire V8. 10-inch semi-centrifugal diaphragm spring type with Super Turbo-Fire V8. 10½-inch semi-centrifugal diaphragm spring type with Turbo-Thrust V8, Super Turbo-Thrust V8, and special V8 engines.

CHASSIS—SAFETY-GIRDER FRAME: Rigid, tunnel-center X-built. FULL COIL SUSPENSION: Four coil springs with double-acting shock absorbers and built-in levelizing action front and rear. Ride stabilizer on all except 6-cylinder Bel Air and Biscayne models. WHEELS AND TIRES: 14″ wheels, 7.50 x 14 4-ply rating blackwall tubeless tires (8.00 x 14 4-ply rating on Convertible and Station Wagons). SAFETY-MASTER BRAKES: 11″ hydraulic, bonded linings, 199.5 sq. in. area. Foot-operated mechanical parking brake. STEERING: Precision Ball-Race gear, overall ratio 28:1 standard, 24:1 with power steering*. REAR AXLE: Hypoid, semi-floating, four ratios tailored to power teams. FUEL CAPACITY: Station Wagons, 17 gals. (except Kingswood, 18 gals.), all others 20 gals. ELECTRICAL: 12-volt system, 30-ampere generator (35-amp. with special V8 engines), 54-plate battery (66-plate with 348 cu. in. V8).

DIMENSIONS—Wheelbase, 119″. Front and rear tread, 60.3″ and 59.3″. Overall: length 210.8″, width 80.8″, height—Sport Sedan and Sport Coupe 54.0″, Convertible and Sedans 56.0″, Station Wagons 56.3″.

OPTIONAL EQUIPMENT—Power steering. Power brakes. Power windows**. Flexomatic 6-Way** or 4-Way** power front seat. Power tailgate window**. Vented full wheel covers. Heavy-duty rear coil springs. Positraction rear axle. Heavy-duty clutch**. Temperature controlled fan. E-Z-Eye glass. Padded instrument panel. De luxe steering wheel**. Foam cushioned front seat**. Heater and defroster. Air conditioner**. Whitewall tires. 8.00 x 14 4-ply black tires**. Choice of radios. Dual exhaust**. Heavy-duty generator. Heavy-duty battery. Two-speed electric windshield wiper and pushbutton windshield washer. Non-glare inside rearview mirror. Oil filter and oil-bath air cleaner for Hi-Thrift 6. Special police or taxicab equipment. Full line of Custom Feature accessories.

*Optional at extra cost.   **Availability determined by either model or equipment.

All illustrations and specifications contained in this literature are based on the latest product information available at the time of publication approval. The right is reserved to make changes at any time without notice in prices, colors, materials, equipment, specifications and models, and also to discontinue models.

CHEVROLET MOTOR DIVISION · GENERAL MOTORS CORPORATION, DETROIT 2, MICHIGAN

Industry sales dipped in 1961. Chevrolet remained strong with calendar year sales of 1.6 million, although that was disappointing when compared to 1960 sales of 1.8 million.

After a one year hiatus where only slight body changes were made, Chevrolet once again introduced an all-new body. Fins were gone for good. The only suggestion that they ever existed remained in the unbroken trim line of chrome molding (without chrome on the Biscayne) that ran from behind the headlights across the slight overhang of the rear deck. The Impala remained a separate series with five models. The Impala retained its visual identity by the triple taillight arrangement, nonfunctional air scoops below the rear window and the crossed flags with Impala nameplate in the side molding inset. Crossed flags were also located on the rear deck lid. The Nomad continued to be the station wagon version of the Impala.

The Impala interior again received a more luxurious level of trim and better quality fabrics and material. Except for the aluminum front seat end panels and the now-traditional arm-rest safety reflectors, there was not much unique to the interior.

A minor downsizing of the line occurred this year. Length was decreased to 209.3", width was chopped to 78.4" and height was a standard 55.5" on all but the station wagons and convertible, which were 56". Powerplant and powertrain options remained virtually the same this year although it would be the last year for the Turboglide transmission. The exciting news, however, was the introduction of the 409 cu. in. V-8. Although it was created from a bored-out, stroked 348 and was never produced in quantity, in years to come this engine would make its mark. It was rated at 360-hp and could clock a quarter-mile in 13.9 seconds with a zero to 60 time of 5.75 seconds. This engine was also the basis for the introduction of the first Chevrolet Super Sport: the Impala SS.

The Impala SS this year was an option available on any Impala model for $53.80. The option included SS identification on the rear quarter panel molding and rear deck, a column-mounted tachometer (virtually useless unless you were turning the steering wheel so that you could see it!), special wheels, padded instrument panel and a passenger assist bar. This latter feature has been compared with the assist bar on the Corvette. The passenger assist bar was also used on the Chevrolet-based Canadian Pontiac Parisienne in 1959. Due to the close association between Chevy models and Canadian Pontic models during the 60's it is possible that some of the inspiration for this came from Canada. The SS was available with 305-, 340-, 350-, or 409-hp engines. A four-speed transmission was the only transmission available except that Powerglide could be specified with the 305-hp engine. Bucket seats were not an available option. The most powerful combination available was an SS with a 409 V-8 equipped with RPO1108, which included a police option chassis with stiffer springs, heavy-duty shocks and large stabilizer bars.

Model year production by body style was: 4d Sdn, 452,251; Spts Cpe, 177,969; Spts Sdn, 174,141; 4d Wgn, 168,935; 2d Sdn, 153,988; Convrtbl, 64,624. Estimated series production made was: Biscayne Fleetmaster, 3,000; Biscayne, 201,000; Bel Air, 330,000; Impala, 491,000. We do have separate information that 453 Impala SS's were built during 1961. Of these, 142 were equipped with the 409 engine.

The least expensive Chevrolet (passenger car not including station wagons) was the Biscayne two-door sedan with a base price of $2,369 (3,425 lbs.) and the most expensive was the Impala Convertible with a base price of $2,954 (3,600 lbs.). The two-door Bel Air sedan was base priced at $2,491 (3,435 lbs.) and the Impala two-door sedan was $2,643 (3,440 lbs.).

Literature this year consisted of the full-line Chevrolet catalogue in oversized format (page 64) and a reduced-size version of it (pages 62-63). Reproduced in this book on pages 60-61 is the first SS brochure. This extremely rare piece of sales literature is interesting in that even in it the availability of the 409 was not announced.

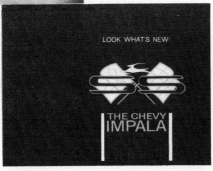

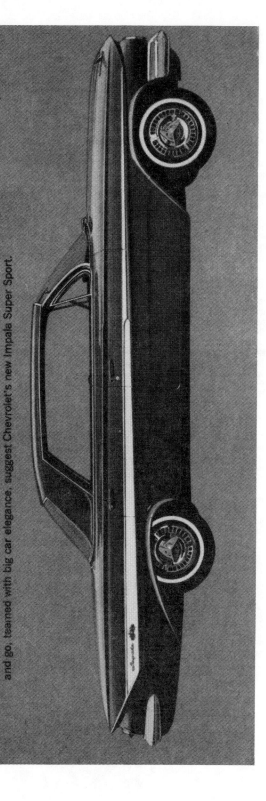

see how much extra the Impala Super Sport* offers

■ Choice of 305-, 340- or 350-h.p. V8 with 4-Speed Synchro-Mesh Transmission (305-h.p. Engine also available with High-Performance Powerglide) ■ Sports Car Front Passenger Assist Bar ■ Electric Tachometer ■ Padded Instrument Panel ■ Special Full Wheel Covers with Simulated Knockoff Hubs ■ Exclusive Super Sport 8.00 x 14 Four-Ply Narrow-Band Whitewall Tires ■ Power Steering ■ Power Brakes ■ Sintered-Metallic Brake Linings ■ Heavy-Duty Front and Rear Coil Springs and Shock Absorbers to assure true sports car handling and roadability ■ Distinctive Super Sport Identification (SS over Exterior Crossed Flags, also SS Assist Bar Emblem).

plus all the elegant standards in every '61 Impala

*A complete special package . . . optional at extra cost for any of the five '61 Impala models.

A VERY SPECIAL VERSION IN CHEVROLET'S MOST LUXURIOUS LINE!

Super Sport is the highly personalized Impala that blends Chevy's full-size, top-of-the-line luxury with a peak performance power team and true sports car equipment. There's a choice of three top-powered V8's (all over 300 h.p.) plus sports-minded interior richness, competition-type suspension and brakes, distinctive "SS" identification inside and out. It's a complete special package available in Chevy's Convertible or any other luxurious '61 Impala model. For discriminating customers who like sports car flair and go, teamed with big car elegance, suggest Chevrolet's new Impala Super Sport.

PEAK PERFORMANCE · SPORTS CAR FEATURES

PERSONALIZED INTERIOR LUXURY! Take a close look at Impala Super Sport's padded instrument panel. Notice how the tachometer (mounted on steering column) and passenger assist bar add real sports car flavor to Impala's tasteful instrument Console design. Check, too, the bright metal Super Sport emblem on the assist bar. Of course, there's all the interior luxury found in every '61 Impala, including full deep-twist carpeting, extra-long armrests and fingertip door releases, foam cushioned seating comfort front and rear.

POWER-PACKED CHOICES! With Impala Super Sport, your customers have Chevy's special 348-cu.-in. V8's to choose from—350, 340 and 305 h.p. There's triple two-barrel carburetion for extra top-end boost in the 350 h.p., four-barrel performance in the other two. All come equipped with dual exhausts and special heavy-duty components. Buyers can team any of these power-packed engines with Chevy's versatile 4-Speed transmission. If they prefer automatic shifting, the 305 h.p. version also can be matched with high-performance Powerglide.

COMPETITION-STYLED FEATURES! Whether your prospect is a staunch enthusiast or just someone who yearns for the sports car approach, he'll go for Impala Super Sport. Take these special wheel covers, for example, with the kind of styling that gives a competition-car look. And those narrow-band whitewall tires are exclusive Super Sport extras, offered with no other full-size Chevy. Underneath, heavy-duty springing and shock absorbers help the Impala Super Sport corner and handle like the best of the world's road champions.

4-SPEED TRANSMISSION! For exhilarating fun and true sports car feel to shifting, Chevy's 4-Speed Synchro-Mesh transmission can't be beat. It has a floor-mounted shift lever, is fully synchronized in all forward speeds for smooth up- and down-shifting. And when customers choose the 4-Speed in an Impala Super Sport, there's an identifying trim plate of bright metal at the shift-lever base. Show your prospects all the special features they can enjoy in the Impala Super Sport. At first chance, let them drive one and experience its exciting difference!

IMPALA SERIES

MOST LUXURIOUS CHEVROLET—You'd be hard-pressed to find a reason for wanting any more car than this! The elegant Impala is unquestionably the finest car in its field. For 1961, a new 2-Door Sedan joins the Impala Series, featuring the new canopy roof and slim pillar sedan styling. Impala standard equipment includes such luxury features as electric clock, parking brake warning light, back-up lights, rich deep-twist carpeting, de luxe window cranks, fingertip door releases and extra long armrests with built-in safety reflectors. Interiors are available in six beautiful color combinations.

IMPALA SPORT COUPE
IN HONDURAS MAROON

Ask about the IMPALA SUPER SPORT*! It's the highly personalized version of any model in Chevy's top luxury line. Just check its great performance rundown: your choice of 305-, 340- or 350-h.p. V8 with 4-Speed Synchro-Mesh transmission (305-h.p. V8 also available with high-performance Powerglide), power steering, power brakes, sintered-metallic brake linings, exclusive 8.00 x 14 narrow-band whitewall tires. There's a distinctive sports car assist bar on the padded instrument panel, electric tachometer, stylish SS identification, full wheel covers with simulated knockoff hubs and heavy-duty suspension components. Get full details at your Chevy dealer's...on the Super Sport, the extra-luxury, higher performance optional package available on all five Impala models.
*Optional at extra cost.

IMPALA SPORT SEDAN IN ARBOR GREEN

IMPALA 4-DOOR SEDAN IN SATEEN SILVER

IMPALA CONVERTIBLE IN SEAMIST TURQUOISE

IMPALA 2-DOOR SEDAN IN CORONNA CREAM

PERFORMANCE–ECONOMY

TRADITIONAL ECONOMY LEADER—Chevy's HI-THRIFT 6 is the industry's most thoroughly refined 6-cylinder design. It gives you proven operating economy from the word go! The Hi-Thrift 6 squeezes extra miles from each gallon . . . runs like a charm on regular gas. Standard automatic choke gives you all the fuel you need for cold-engine starts . . . thriftily leans the mixture the instant the engine is warm. Advanced hydraulic valve lifters give quieter operation . . . never need adjusting. Economical 8.25 to 1 compression ratio . . . lively 135-h.p. rating.

A WIDE RANGE OF V8'S—ECONOMY TURBO-FIRE V8 makes gas saving a V8 virtue! This standard V8 engine features an economy-contoured camshaft that gives more torque, more efficient operation, in the low and middle speed ranges you use most. A finely calibrated 2-barrel carburetor also helps mete out the fuel in miserly fashion. Still another money-saving feature: this husky engine delivers its V8 "go" on regular gas! Cylinder head design helps boost oil economy. Full-flow oil filter is standard equipment. 283-cu.-in. displacement, 8.5 to 1 compression ratio, 170 h.p.

Four-barrel carburetion gives Chevy's 283-cu.-in. SUPER TURBO-FIRE V8* an extra measure of get-up-and-go whenever the occasion calls for it. At normal driving speeds you operate economically on just 2 barrels. 9.5 to 1 compression ratio, 230 horsepower.

Chevy's 348-cu.-in. TURBO-THRUST V8* is sized and equipped for performance! Its wedge-shaped combustion chambers are precision machined to deliver smooth, quiet power . . . efficient fuel burning. Four-barrel carburetor, high-efficiency air cleaner and dual exhaust system are standard equipment. Compression ratio, 9.5 to 1; 250 h.p.

Triple two-barrel carburetion puts extra muscle in the 348-cu.-in. SUPER TURBO-THRUST V8*. At normal cruising speeds you run on just two barrels, but when you need peak performance just step down on the accelerator and all six barrels go into action. Dual exhausts are standard. Compression ratio, 9.5 to 1; 280 h.p.

5 FINE TRANSMISSIONS

Standard equipment on every Chevrolet is 3-SPEED SYNCHRO-MESH . . . as smoothly coordinated and dependable a manual shift as any ever made. Chevrolet OVERDRIVE* will give you top economy over the long haul. It cuts the number of engine revolutions for each turn of the wheels . . . reduces engine wear, saves on gas. You can select 4-SPEED SYNCHRO-MESH* as a performance partner for any one of Chevy's spirited 348-cu.-in. V8's. It has a floor-mounted shift lever, and is fully synchronized in all forward speeds for smooth up- and down-shifting.

For the most popular automatic transmission in the low-price field, look no farther than Chevrolet's POWERGLIDE!* Its low initial cost, dependability and liquid-smooth shifting have made it the

SELECT FROM THE INDUSTRY'S WIDEST CHOICE OF POWER TEAMS

	Turboglide	Powerglide	4-Speed Synchro-Mesh	3-Speed Synchro-Mesh	Overdrive
280-h.p. Super Turbo-Thrust V8**	X		X	X	
250-h.p. Turbo-Thrust V8**†	X		X	X	
230-h.p. Super Turbo-Fire V8	X	X		X	X
170-h.p. Economy Turbo-Fire V8	X	X		X	X
135-h.p. Hi-Thrift 6		X		X	X

**These two engines, modified for special uses, are available with power ratings of 350 h.p. and 340 h.p. respectively, with either 3-Speed or 4-Speed Synchro-Mesh transmissions. †Also 305 h.p. available with heavy-duty Powerglide, and 3-Speed or 4-Speed Synchro-Mesh transmissions.

biggest selling automatic in its class. For the ultimate, try TURBOGLIDE.* With its triple-turbine action, you never feel a shift in "Drive"—the only sensation is a whisper-smooth flow of power. Chevy's built-in grade retarder provides an exclusive assist in downhill braking.

CHEVY OPTIONS AND POWER FEATURES

POWER STEERING* is virtually effortless, instantly responsive. It makes highway driving safer . . . parking so much easier. And Power Steering will return a good portion of your investment at trade-in time. **POWER BRAKES*** relieve you of up to one-third of the braking effort . . . give an extra measure of safety in an emergency. This low-cost power feature will repay you in comfort many times over. **POWER WINDOWS*** operate from a master control on the driver's door . . . eliminate reaching. For passenger convenience there is also a push button for each window. **6-WAY FLEXOMATIC POWER SEAT*** moves forward and back, up and down, even tilts to the most comfortable angle . . . all at the touch of a button. **AIR CONDITIONING*** gives you four-season temperature control inside your Chevrolet. Chevrolet Air Conditioning operates in conjunction with the heater, giving warm air in winter . . . cool, dry, pollen- and dust-free air in summer. **NEW DE LUXE HEATER*** improves temperature control through a new air blending system. Temperature setting controls the amount of cold and hot air mixed . . . allows an infinite variation in temperature and registers new temperature settings immediately. **POSITRACTION REAR AXLE*** automatically transfers power to the wheel with the grip. All you need is one rear wheel with traction, and Positraction will keep you going through sand, mud, ice and snow.

*Optional at extra cost.

In an upbeat year for industry sales in general, Chevrolet's calendar year production leapt almost 556,000 units. Impala accounted for almost 40% of this increase (the new Chevy II accounted for virtually all the rest).

One look at the new sheet metal and styling showed why this year was so popular. This would be the first year that the Impala SS began to be recognized by the buying public. It was available as an option on either the Impala Convertible or Sport Coupe. With the Sport Coupe, it shared the new roof line of the GM B-Body cars. The subtle shape of the roof gave a convertible flair to this hard top. Nomad station wagons disappeared this year and in their place a station wagon wore the Impala nameplate. Other major changes to the line included the elimination of the never-popular Biscayne Fleetmaster series and produce the last year of the Bel Air Sport Coupe. All of the station wagons carried only the series names: Biscayne, Bel Air and Impala.

The Impala SS was the big news, of course. This beautiful package came with the same interior trim as its 1961 predecessor but added bucket seats with a flip-top center console. The column-mounted tachometer disappeared as part of the standard package. Exterior SS identification was made by the tri-blade spinner wheelcovers, the "SS" letters which overlay the standard Impala emblem on the rear fenders and the Super Sport identification on the rear quarter panel.

This year there were no powerplant restrictions with the SS option. You could have an SS with the 235 six if you were Philistine enough. The most popular variations were, of course, the V-8 in either 327 or 409 form. The 327 proved to be immensely popular. While the rodders had been boring out the venerable 283 for years, Chevy created the 327 with a 1/8" overbore and a 1/4" stroke adjustment. The 327 replaced the 348 V-8 and was available in 250-hp or 300-hp with 4-bbl carbs and 10.5:1 compression. The hot 409, which kept getting hotter during the model year with revised cams and heads, was available in 380-hp with 4-bbl carbs and 409-hp with dual 4-bbl carbs. Both had 11:1 compression.

Length was 209.6", width was 79" and height 55" for the convertible, 56" for station wagons and 55.5" for the others. Production figures were again issued by Chevrolet by body type (excluding Chevy II): 4d Sdn, 533,349; Spts Cpe, 323,427; 4d Wgn, 187,566; Spts Sdn, 176,077; 2d Sdn, 127,870; Convtbl, 75,719. Other sources estimate model production (rounded to nearest 100) at: Biscayne, 166,000 (30,400 with V-8); Bel Air, 365,500 (169,000 with V-8); Impala 704,900 (596,200 with V-8) of which 99,311 were equipped with the SS option; station wagons 187,600 (126,300 with V-8). Total cars equipped with the 409 engine are reported to have been 15,019.

The least expensive Chevrolet (passenger car excluding station wagons) was the Biscayne two-door sedan with a base price of $2,431 (3,400 lbs.) and the most expensive was the Impala Convertible with a base price of $3,026 (3,560 lbs.). The Bel Air two-door sedan was base priced at $2,563 (3,405 lbs.) and the four-door Impala sedan was base priced at $2,769 (3,505 lbs.).

Literature this year consisted of the full-line Chevrolet catalogue (page 69) and the standard-size Chevys catalogue (pages 68,70-72). Chevrolet began to promote performance in its magazine ads this year for the first time in several seasons (pages 66-67).

1962

NOBODY KNOWS ENTHUSIASTS
AS WELL AS CHEVROLET

After all, who introduced the four-speed all-synchro transmission (one of the world's best) in American cars? Chevy. Who started the recent trend to bucket seats? Chevy did. Who built a real honest-to-goodness sports car back when hardly anybody else on this side of the Atlantic even knew what they were? Chevy again. Who pioneered Fuel-Injection for American cars? You guessed it.

Right now, Chevrolet builds a wider variety of models for discerning drivers than anybody, except perhaps a couple of European one-of-a-kind custom builders. Everything from frolicsome two-seaters to full-size family sedans, all available with a fantastic array of equipment designed to suit the more demanding driver.

Imagine a car like the Impala Sport Coupe with such optional-at-extra-cost equipment as bucket seats, four-speed box, 409-cubic-inch engine, Positraction, heavy-duty shocks and springs, and sintered-iron brakes. It'll out-handle and out-run quite a gang of good automobiles, and it'll carry you, your wife, your mother-in-law, two kids, a bird cage and a springer spaniel in the process.

If you're a one-car man with a ten- or twelve-car appetite, try a combination like that —it's not bad, and it'll sure leave a trail of disillusioned sports cars in your wake. Chevrolet Division of General Motors, Detroit 2, Michigan.

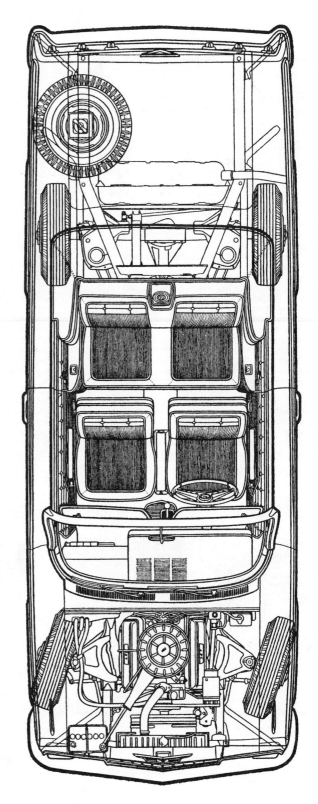

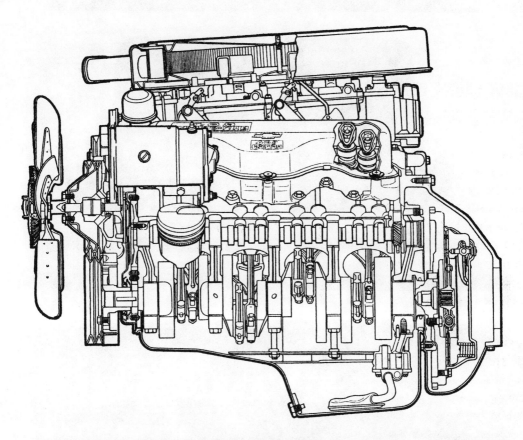

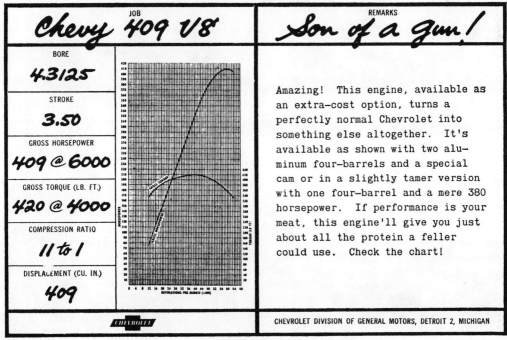

Chevy 409 V8 — JOB

Son of a gun! — REMARKS

BORE

4.3125

STROKE

3.50

GROSS HORSEPOWER

409 @ 6000

GROSS TORQUE (LB. FT.)

420 @ 4000

COMPRESSION RATIO

11 to 1

DISPLACEMENT (CU. IN.)

409

Amazing! This engine, available as an extra-cost option, turns a perfectly normal Chevrolet into something else altogether. It's available as shown with two aluminum four-barrels and a special cam or in a slightly tamer version with one four-barrel and a mere 380 horsepower. If performance is your meat, this engine'll give you just about all the protein a feller could use. Check the chart!

CHEVROLET

CHEVROLET DIVISION OF GENERAL MOTORS, DETROIT 2, MICHIGAN

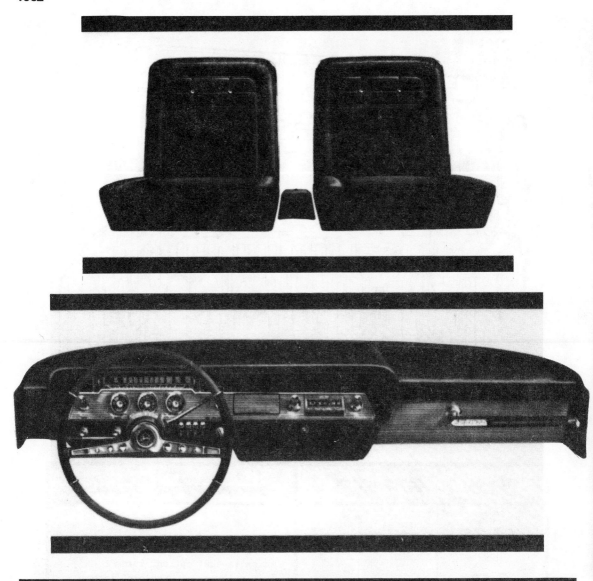

Impala Super Sport . . . personalized version of Chevrolet's most elegant series—Chevrolet's special Impala Super Sport equipment* gives you a unique opportunity to combine sports car style and features with full-size room and comfort. It is available for both the Impala Sport Coupe and Impala Convertible, with either standard 6 or V8, and includes: front bucket seats; leather-soft vinyl throughout; sports car assist bar; between-seat console with locking compartment; patterned aluminum body side molding insert; wheel covers with knock-off hub styling; plus distinctive Super Sport identification. You can gear up the go to match the sporty look with Chevrolet's many performance options*. Choose from one of Chevrolet's four optional V8's (ranging from 250 hp to 409 hp) and such high-performance equipment as 4-Speed Synchro-Mesh transmission, sintered-metallic brake linings, heavy-duty springs and shocks, 8.00 x 14 tires and electric tachometer.

*Optional at extra cost.

'62 CHEVROLET

RICH NEW STYLING WITH A JET-SMOOTH RIDE! If you like a big car, you'll find the new Chevrolet more to your liking every time. When you look it over, the sculptured styling stands out fresh and luxurious from any angle. When you enter it (with ease through big wide-opening doors), you discover a new interior elegance and spacious, relaxing comfort. Take a Jet-smooth ride in the '62 Chevrolet. Sit back and let its husky Full Coil suspension smooth away the road shocks. You're sure to appreciate the regular-gas savings you can get from its refined 170-hp Turbo-Fire 283 or 135-hp Hi-Thrift 235. Not to mention the lasting beauty of its Magic-Mirror finish and famous durability of its Body by Fisher. (Even unique inner fenders up front this year to protect vital parts.) All told, the full-sized '62 Chevrolet is like owning an expensive car but without its expense. Choose from 14 beautiful new models—Impalas, Bel Airs and Biscaynes. Each series, by the way, now includes Station Wagons!

IMPALA

MOST ELEGANT CAR OF ITS KIND! A rare combination of qualities marks this year's Impala as the finest investment in its class. Interiors are the most luxurious ever offered. Distinctive styling gives a new overall look of richness. (You see this most dramatically in the roof line flair of the Sport Coupe.) More choices than ever before, too. Six in all, the 4 you see here plus the 4-Door Sedan and 4-Door 9-Passenger Station Wagon. There's even a Super Sport version, with front bucket seats and special features, available* in the Impala Sport Coupe and Convertible models. And every '62 Impala incorporates all the reasons that make a Chevrolet traditionally hold a higher resale value than other makes. For top elegance in Chevrolet's big-car line, look over the '62 Impala!

IMPALA SPORT COUPE in Autumn Gold. Glamorous new combination . . . the luxury of a hardtop with the look of a convertible!

IMPALA INTERIOR. You'd be hard put to find more elegance than you get here. Fact is, you usually find luxury like this only in higher priced cars. Upholstery blends rich patterned fabrics and soft leather-grain vinyl. Trimmed with bright metal buttoning and deep-tufted squares. Beautiful color combinations—in fawn, aqua, red, blue, green and gold—are keyed to your choice of 14 exterior colors. New Impala Convertible even comes in a black interior and gives you the practicality of all-vinyl seat coverings. In every '62 Impala, other luxuries that enhance the interior are full deep-twist carpeting, bright metal end-trim on the front seat, plus an exclusively fashioned steering wheel and instrument panel trim. *Optional at extra cost*

Shown on front cover from top to bottom: CORVAIR MONZA CLUB COUPE in Roman Red. CHEVY II NOVA 400 SPORT COUPE in Autumn Gold. CHEVROLET IMPALA SPORT COUPE in Twilight Turquoise.

'62 CHEVROLET

Power Teams

a choice for every driving need

Again in '62, Chevrolet offers a wide range of engines and transmissions to help you build a power team specifically for your kind of driving. And many of the engines and transmissions you'll want to choose from are new designs for 1962. Check this run-down on Chevrolet power teams—consult the handy power team chart to see how you can fit one to your needs.

6 ENGINES

135-hp Hi-Thrift 235. This famous Chevrolet 6 has proved its dependability and economy over many millions of owner-driven miles. Among its outstanding features are precision-balanced forged steel crankshaft (for smoother operation, long life), standard automatic choke and advanced valve-in-head design featuring hydraulic valve lifters that never need adjusting. '62 improvements: a new oil-wetted air filter made of easy-to-clean polyurethane and a new partial-flow oil filter as standard equipment. Compression ratio: 8.25 to 1.

170-hp Turbo-Fire 283. Chevrolet's standard V8 engine combines lively V8 performance with budget-watching fuel economy. Its economy-contoured camshaft delivers more torque—more efficient performance—in the low and middle speed ranges where most of your driving is done. A thrifty 2-barrel carburetor helps squeeze more miles out of every gallon of money-saving regular gas. This year automatic choke operation has been made even more reliable. And a new air cleaner inlet quiets the flow of air for the carburetor. Other standard equipment features include hydraulic valve lifters, positive-shift starter and full-flow oil filter. Displacement: 283 cu. in. Compression ratio: 8.5 to 1.

250-hp Turbo-Fire 327.* Here's a totally new 327-cu.-in. V8 engine for '62. It's light in weight, with high power output—resulting in new operating efficiency and outstanding performance. Cast iron cylinder heads of new composition give greater strength. Special water passages

provide better spark plug cooling. Full-pressure lubrication system with full-flow oil filter, 4-barrel carburetor, hydraulic valve lifters, automatic choke, dry-type air cleaner and dual exhausts with resonators are all standard equipment. Compression ratio: 10.5 to 1.

300-hp Turbo-Fire 327.* Refinements boost the power output on this modified version of Chevrolet's 327-cu.-in. V8. A larger 4-barrel carburetor (featuring aluminum construction), oversized inlet valves and a larger dual exhaust system provide the key to its 300-hp rating. Compression ratio: 10.5 to 1.

380-hp Turbo-Fire 409.* This is a husky 409-cu.-in. V8 that turns out 420 lb-ft. torque. Special features include a large-throat 4-barrel aluminum carburetor, dual-snorkle air cleaner, large-passage intake manifold, high-performance camshaft with mechanical valve lifters, tough-surface crankshaft bearings and extra-strong pistons. Its cast iron cylinder heads feature large valves and smooth ports. Automatic choke, full-flow oil filter and dual exhausts are standard. Compression ratio: 11.0 to 1.

409-hp Turbo-Fire 409.* Designed for all-out performance at peak engine speeds. Has twin 4-barrel carburetors, large exhaust passages, plus other modifications. Includes all Turbo-Fire 409 features. (8.00 x 14 nylon cord tires* are recommended with all 409-cu.-in. engines.) Compression ratio: 11.0 to 1.

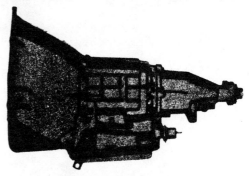

4 TRANSMISSIONS

Standard 3-Speed Synchro-Mesh. This dependable, easy-shifting transmission is standard on all Chevrolet models, and is designed to be teamed with any of Chevrolet's six engines for 1962. Gear ratios matched to engine.

Overdrive.* Chevrolet Overdrive will help you get the top economy the engine is designed to deliver. It cuts the number of engine revolutions for each turn of the wheels, saving gas, reducing engine wear.

4-Speed Synchro-Mesh.* Offered as a high-performance partner with Chevrolet's 327- and 409-cu.-in. engines. Four fully synchronized forward speeds. Down-shifts smoothly at all speeds. Floor-mounted shift lever.

Powerglide.* When you choose Powerglide you get the most dependable, most thoroughly proved automatic transmission available. Among the characteristics which have made Powerglide the biggest selling automatic in its class are low cost, long life and liquid-smooth shifting. A new version, featuring low-weight aluminum construction, will be used with 327-cu.-in. V8 engines for 1962.

1962 CHEVROLET POWER TEAMS				
STANDARD ENGINES	3-SPEED SYNCHRO-MESH	OVERDRIVE*	4-SPEED SYNCHRO-MESH*	POWERGLIDE*
135-hp Hi-Thrift 235	3.36:1 axle**	3.70:1 axle	N.A.	3.36:1 axle
170-hp Turbo-Fire 283	3.36:1 axle	3.70:1 axle	N.A.	3.36:1 axle
OPTIONAL V8's				
250-hp Turbo-Fire 327	3.36:1 axle	N.A.	3.36:1 axle	3.08:1 axle
300-hp Turbo-Fire 327	3.36:1 axle	N.A.	3.36:1 axle	3.36:1 axle
380-hp Turbo-Fire 409	3.36:1 axle	N.A.	3.08:1 axle†	N.A.
409-hp Turbo-Fire 409	3.36:1 axle	N.A.	3.08:1 axle†	N.A.

*Optional at extra cost.
**3.55:1 in Station Wagons. N.A.—Not Available. †3.36:1 with close-ratio trans.

Comfort and Convenience

with '62 Chevrolet options and custom features

Power Steering.* Smooth, almost effortless control that responds instantly to your touch. Hydraulic pressure does up to 80 per cent of the work, takes the chore out of handling and parking. Yet, you still have excellent road feel, even at highway speeds. Low (24:1) overall steering ratio gives quicker response. Coming out of turns, wheel returns smoothly and surely.

Power Brakes.* For 1962, you can put greater stopping ease and safety at the tip of your toe. A large power cylinder increases braking force by up to one-third, with the same pedal pressure. Wide, low pedal assures fast, sure application. Large vacuum reserve supplies braking power even after the engine is shut off.

Power Windows.* A touch of the finger-tip control moves side windows up or down. Electric motor provides quiet power. Driver's master control operates all windows. Passengers have individual control at each window. Available on all Impala and Bel Air models.

6-Way Flexomatic Power Seat.* Versatile, power-operated front seat adjusts to any position. Three-button control panel lets you move the seat fore and aft, up and down, or tilt it forward or back. (Available with all Impala and Bel Air models.)

All-Weather Air Conditioning.* Improved, quieter unit offers year-round driving comfort for any 1962 Chevrolet. Keeps you cool and fresh in summer, warm as toast in winter. System provides de-humidified air that is virtually dust- and pollen-free inside the car. Outlets are located for maximum comfort.

New De Luxe Push-Button Radio.* New all-transistor radio plays the instant you turn it on. Takes 30% less current to operate, is built to deliver longer life. It's acoustically engineered for Chevrolet interiors and features automatic volume control to prevent station fading. Five push buttons can be easily set to any station.

Positraction Rear Axle.* Wherever the footing is unsure —in snow, mud, sand and gravel—Positraction transfers power to the wheel with the grip. Available for all 1962 Chevrolet power teams.

Soft-Ray Tinted Glass.* Helps shield you from the sun's heat and glare—reduces the brilliance of oncoming headlights. Windshields and Bel Air Sport Coupe rear windows feature a graduated dark band at the top to give additional protection against glare from overhead. Soft-Ray tinted glass is available for all windows, or for windshields or Bel Air Sport Coupe rear windows, separately.

*Optional at extra cost.

Body—All-welded Fisher Unisteel construction, sealed and insulated, acoustically hushed, extra-large rubber mountings. Double-walled cowl, extra-heavy side rails and integral body crossmembers. High-Level ventilation and built-in blended-air heater and defroster system. Magic-Mirror acrylic lacquer finish. Crank-operated ventipanes. Roll-down rear window in Station Wagons, power operated in 9-passenger models. Single-key locking system, keyless door locking, pushbutton door handles. Interiors color-keyed to car exterior, all-vinyl sidewall trim.

Biscayne Standard Features—Distinctive trim and identification, dual electric parallel-action windshield wipers, directional signals, enclosed steering column, 17″ recessed-hub steering wheel with horn button, foam-cushioned front seat, front armrests, two coat hooks, dual adjustable sun visors, cigarette lighter, glove compartment lock. Nylon-blend pattern cloth seat upholstery and cloth headlining (pattern vinyl in Station Wagon). Color-keyed vinyl-coated rubber floor mats.

Bel Air Additional Features—Extra-quality trim and identification, foam-cushioned rear seat, nylon-blend pattern cloth seat upholstery. Vinyl headlining in Sport Coupe and Station Wagons, cloth in other models. Recessed-hub steering wheel with dual thumb button horn control, rear armrests, glove compartment light, automatic interior light switches at front doors. Full carpet floor covering and foam-backed fabric luggage compartment mat—plus Biscayne general features.

Impala Additional Features—Luxury trim and distinctive identification, aluminum front seat end panels, extra-long armrests with finger-tip door release. Special sports-styled steering wheel with dual thumb button horn control. Electric clock. Parking brake warning light. Safety reflectors in lower door panels. Rich nylon-blend seat upholstery (pattern vinyl in Convertible), vinyl headlining. Dual backup lights and luggage compartment lamp—plus Biscayne and Bel Air general features. Super Sport equipment including all-vinyl trim, bucket front seats, and other features optional at extra cost for Sport Coupe and Convertible.

Engine—135-hp HI-THRIFT 235: 6-cylinder 235.5-cu.-in. displacement, 8.25:1 compression ratio, single barrel carburetion, single exhaust. 170-hp TURBO-FIRE 283: V8, 283-cu.-in. displacement, 8.5:1 c.r., two-barrel carburetion, single exhaust. 250-hp TURBO-FIRE 327*: V8, 327-cu.-in. displacement, 10.5:1 c.r, four-barrel carburetion, dual exhaust. 300-hp TURBO-FIRE 327*: V8, 327-cu.-in. displacement, 10.5:1 c.r., large four-barrel carburetion, dual exhaust. 380-hp TURBO-FIRE 409*: V8, 409-cu.-in. displacement, 11.0:1 c.r., large four-barrel carburetion, dual exhaust. 409-hp TURBO-FIRE 409*: V8, 409-cu.-in. displacement, 11.0:1 c.r., twin four-barrel carburetion, dual exhaust. 1962 Chevrolet engines feature valve-in-head design, aluminum pistons, forged steel crankshaft, positive-shift starter, and automatic choke. Hydraulic valve lifters on all except 409-cu.-in. V8 engines. Both 409 V8s have special camshaft, mechanical valve lifters and other features. All V8 engines have dry-element type air cleaner, except oil-wetted on 380-hp V8. Full-flow oil filter on all V8 engines. 135-hp Hi-Thrift 235 has oil-wetted air cleaner and partial-flow oil filter. Temperature-controlled viscous drive fan on all 327- and 409-cu.-in. V8 engines.

Transmission—POWERGLIDE*: Two-speed three-element torque converter with hydraulically controlled planetary gears. Positive parking lock. Selector sequence Park-R-N-D-L. 4-SPEED SYNCHRO-MESH*: Aluminum case, helical gear design, all forward gears fully synchronized. Choice of ratios with 409-cu.-in. V8s. Central floor-mounted shift lever. OVERDRIVE*: 3-Speed Synchro-Mesh plus 2-speed planetary overdrive, engaged semi-automatically above approximately 30 m.p.h. 3-SPEED SYNCHRO-MESH: All-helical gear design with high torque capacity. Gear ratios matched to engine.

Clutch—Single plate dry disk with two facings, spring cushioned, permanently lubricated release bearing. 9.5-inch diaphragm spring type with 135-hp Hi-Thrift 235 engine. 10-inch diaphragm spring type with 170-hp Turbo-Fire 283. 10.5-inch diaphragm spring type with 250- and 300-hp Turbo-Fire 327. 10.5-inch semi-centrifugal coil spring type with 380- and 409-hp Turbo-Fire 409 V8 engines.

Chassis—SAFETY-GIRDER FRAME: Rigid, tunnel-center X-built. FULL COIL SUSPENSION: Four coil springs with double-acting shock absorbers and built-in levelizing action front and rear. Ride stabilizer except on 6-cylinder Bel Air and Biscayne Sedans and Bel Air Sport Coupe. WHEELS AND TIRES: 14″ wheels, 7.50 x 14 blackwall tubeless tires—exceptions: 7.00 x 14 on Biscayne Sedans with standard 6 or V8 engines and manual-shift transmissions; 8.00 x 14 on all Station Wagons and with 409-cu.-in. V8 engines. SAFETY-MASTER BRAKES: 11″ hydraulic, bonded linings, 199.5-sq.-in. area. Foot-operated mechanical parking brake. STEERING: Precision Ball-Race gear, overall ratio 28:1 standard, 24:1 with power steering*. REAR AXLE: Hypoid, semi-floating, four ratios tailored to power teams. FUEL CAPACITY: Station Wagons, 19 gallons, all others 20 gallons. ELECTRICAL: 12-volt system, 30-ampere generator (35-amp. with 409-cu.-in. V8 engines), 54-plate battery (66-plate with 327- and 409-cu.-in. V8 engines).

Dimensions—Wheelbase, 119″. Front and rear tread, 60.3″ and 59.3″. Overall: length 209.6″, width 79.0″, height—Convertible 55.0″, Station Wagons 56.0″, all others 55.5″.

Optional Equipment*—Power steering. Power brakes. Power windows**. Flexomatic 6-way power front seat**. Power tailgate window (Standard on 9-Passenger Wagons). Station Wagon split second seat and lock for concealed stowage compartment. Seat belts. Vented full wheel covers. Heavy-duty springs. Heavy-duty shock absorbers**. Positraction rear axle. Heavy-duty clutch**. Temperature controlled fan**. Heavy-duty radiator. Special sintered-metallic brake linings. Soft-Ray tinted glass. Padded instrument panel. De luxe steering wheel**. Extra-heavy foam-cushioned front seat**. All-Weather** or Cool-Pack air conditioner. Two-Tone finish**. Super Sport Equipment**. Comfort and Convenience Equipment. Front Grille Guard. Rear Bumper Guards**. Whitewall tires. Oversize and special tires**. Pushbutton or manual radio and antenna. Heavy-duty generator** or Delcotrons. Heavy-duty battery. Two-speed electric windshield wipers and pushbutton washer. Tachometer**. Crankcase ventilation equipment. Economy carburetor for 135-hp Hi-Thrift 235. Special police or taxicab equipment**. Full line of Custom Feature accessories.

*Optional at extra cost.   **Availability determined by either model or equipment.

Although industry sales did not repeat the giant leap forward made the previous year, calendar year production was up for Chevrolet by about 140,000 units.

The Impala was mildly restyled this year. Amber parking lights were installed for the first time and the grille was extended completely across the front. Side trim was changed eliminating the wheel house molding. The body beltline molding was lowered and appeared to rest on the rear wheel house running from the rear bumper to just behind the front wheel house. Twin parallel bars rested on the front quarter panel above the bumper edge. The Impala symbol was housed on the upper rear quarter panel while the "Impala" letters appeared in the wide area of the side trim. The rear deck was modified and created a slightly more boxey look than in 1962. Vinyl roofing was available for the first time as an option. The nonfunctional air scoops below the rear window disappeared. Chevrolet included a new flush-and-dry ventilation system designed to minimize rocker panel rust.

Exterior SS identification was limited this year to the "SS" letters superimposed on the Impala symbol and special wheelcovers which contained the red-filled SS letters. The SS was basically a trim option since no power teams were unique to it. The interior provided bucket seats with locking center console and SS identification. The passenger assist bar was deleted. The instrument panel was attractively redesigned with swirl-pattern aluminum inserts. The SS option added $156 to the price of an Impala.

With the Sport Coupe eliminated from the line-up, the Bel Air was down to two models, as was the Biscayne (plus wagons).

Length increased to 210.4" while height remained the same at 79". That there was big news on the power front was not surprising. That the news included something interesting with the venerable standard six was surprising. The old 235 was replaced with a 230 cu. in. 140-hp version. The V-8 line-up was expanded in mid-year to include a 430-hp 427 V-8 (RPO Z11) as the top-of-the-line power producer. (This engine should not be confused with the "Daytona Mystery Engine" of which about five were made). At model year introduction the largest engine was the 425-hp 409 with dual 4-bbl carburetion and 11:1 compression. Powerglide transmission was available on all but the top-rated engines.

Production by body style was: 4d Sdn, 561,511; Spts Cpe, 399,224; 4d Wgn, 198,542; Spts Sdn, 194,158; 2d Sdn, 135,636; Convtbl, 82,659. Estimated production by series: Biscayne, 186,500 (37,000 with V-8); Bel Air, 354,100 (177,200 with V-8); Impala, 832,600 (735,900 with V-8 and 153,2712 with SS equipment); station wagons, 198,500 (146,200 with V-8).

The lowest priced Chevrolet this year (excluding station wagons) was the two-door Biscayne sedan with a base price of $2,429 (3,340 lbs.) and the most expensive was the Impala Convertible with a base price of $3,024 (3,525 lbs.). The two-door Bel Air sedan was base priced at $2,561 (3,345 lbs.) and the Impala four-door sedan carried a base tag of $2,768 (3,435 lbs.).

Literature this year consisted of the full-line catalogue and the big Chevrolets catalogue (pages 74-75 and 78). There was also an little mailer catalogue entitled, "Go The Chevy Fun Route For 1963" which encouraged you to go north, south, east or west so long as you did it in a Chevrolet. This brochure used a nice illustration of an Impala SS (page 77). Another mailer, a folder entitled, "Great Ways to Go 'His' and 'Hers' for 1963!" also featured the Impala SS (page 76).

'63 CHEVROLET

CLEAN-CUT AS A JEWEL, SMOOTH-RIDING AS A JET

Set yourself a standard for full-size value and watch the Jet-smooth '63 Chevrolet more than measure up to it. Clean, refreshing style fairly sparkles with a new brand of beauty. Elegantly fashioned interiors are smartly trimmed in rich new fabrics. Famous Jet-smooth ride *still* flattens out those bumpy roads. And beneath Chevrolet's good looks, there's a big bundle of money-saving benefits that make owning and driving this new Chevrolet more of a pleasure. Easy-care chassis items like self-adjusting Safety-Master brakes and a new battery-saving Delcotron generator. A new standard 6 and improved standard V8 engine that thrive on regular gas. And '63 Chevrolet is true to its heritage. Throughout, you'll find the same careful concern for craftsmanship, the same engineering excellence that have made Chevrolet the most consistent favorite of Americans for decades. These are just a few of the many reasons why Chevrolet's resale value is traditionally high and why owning a Chevrolet is such a wise investment. Again offered in the three familiar series—Impala, Bel Air and Biscayne—but each giving a bigger measure of value than ever before.

SUPER SPORT EQUIPMENT

An Impala Series special is the Super Sport* version. Front bucket seats, distinctive identification, bright aluminum body trim and smart wheel covers set it in a class apart. Super Sport equipment is available on Impala Sport Coupe or Convertible and includes special coil springs. You can match its sporty style with Chevrolet's many performance options*.

*Optional at extra cost.

Front cover: Impala Sport Sedan in Palomar Red

Copyright 1962, Chevrolet Motor Division, General Motors Corp.

Impala Super Sport Coupe in Cordovan Brown.

You'll wonder where the effort went when you take over the family driving chores in the full-size '63 Chevrolet. That's because Chevrolet handles so wonderfully smooth and easy on the highway or in heavy traffic. One reason: Chevrolet's easy-acting, almost effortless and frictionless Ball-Race steering gear. The next best thing to power steering, it makes parking and handling easy. Nearly chair-high seats let you sit up in a comfortable natural position. The steering wheel is placed at an ideal angle for maximum driving ease and comfort. This gives you a satisfying feeling of complete mastery at all times. And '63 Chevrolet makes it easy for you to look and act like the lady you are. Door openings are wide and high for the

kind of entry and exit room you want and need, whether you're wearing a tight skirt or sporting your Sunday-best bonnet. And you'll find a generous expanse of head and leg room in every model.

GO WEST

THE JET-SMOOTH CHEVROLET WAY

There's plenty of room to roam in the scenic West. But before you decide to leave, check your Chevrolet dealer and see if it wouldn't be more fun going in one of the spirited new Chevrolets: Impalas, Bel Airs and Biscaynes. Overall, your choice in convertible, hardtops, sedans, station wagons and the added sporting flair of the Impala Super Sports*. Take a look inside. Rich color-keyed upholsteries blend with one of Chevrolet's 15 solid color or 11 two-tone Magic-Mirror finishes. Select from a wide range of pep and economy with 4 transmissions (3- and 4-Speed* Synchro-Mesh, Overdrive* or automatic Powerglide*) and 7 engines (including the new standard 140-hp Turbo-Thrift 230 six and the 340-hp Turbo-Fire 409 V8*). You'll go for the easy-care maintenance items, too. Safety-Master self-adjusting brakes, extended-life exhaust system and Delcotron generator can offer convenience and savings. Full Coil suspension, Safety-Girder X-built frame and Ball-Race steering give you the easiest handling Jet-smooth ride since the buckboard first got springs. And you'll probably have a heap of praise for such features as the optional new Comfortilt Steering Wheel* (adjustable to 7 positions) and power steering*, brakes*, windows*, and front seat*.

*Optional at extra cost. Check your Chevrolet dealer for exact model availability.

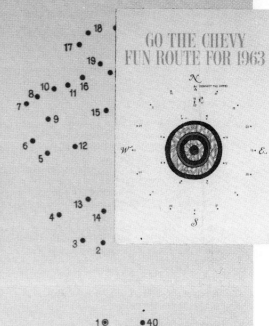

Impala Super Sport Convertible in Palomar Red

SEVEN ENGINES

NEW STANDARD 140-HP TURBO-THRIFT 230—For '63, Chevrolet draws on its unmatched experience as the world's leading producer of 6-cylinder engines to bring you considerably improved gasoline economy. Chevrolet's new 6 is compactly designed, lighter in weight, more efficient and more economical. Thin-wall design for cylinder head and block keeps weight to a minimum. Modified-wedge combustion chambers. Short-stroke design. Seven main bearings for exceptional sturdiness. Full-pressure lubrication. New automatic choke for more precise response to engine temperature. 230-cu.-in. displacement, 8.5:1 compression ratio, single-barrel carburetor, oil-wetted air cleaner and full-flow oil filter.

IMPROVED STANDARD 195-HP TURBO-FIRE 283—Design changes provide 25 more horsepower and contribute to improved economy. Operates on regular grade fuel. Higher lift camshaft opens intake and exhaust valves farther for better engine breathing, greater flow of fuel-air mixture to combustion chambers. Slightly smaller combustion chambers squeeze fuel-air mixture tighter, help increase compression ratio. Two-barrel carburetor, full-pressure lubrication, 283-cu.-in. displacement. 9.25:1 compression ratio, dry-element air cleaner.

250-HP TURBO-FIRE 327*—Low weight-to-output ratio for operating efficiency and performance. Temperature-controlled fan. Full-pressure lubrication system with full-flow oil filter. Hydraulic valve lifters, automatic choke, dry-element air cleaner. 327-cu.-in. displacement, 10.5:1 compression ratio, four-barrel carburetor, dual exhaust. Positive crankcase ventilation (all Chevrolet engines for '63).

300-HP TURBO-FIRE 327*—Refined version of Chevrolet's 327-cu.-in. V8 with big aluminum-body four-barrel carburetor. Large inlet valves. 327-cu.-in. displacement, 10.5:1 compression ratio, large diameter dual exhaust system.

NEW 340-HP TURBO-FIRE 409*—An engine for modern traffic use. New 340-hp 409-cu.-in. V8 has high torque characteristics. Single four-barrel carburetor, hydraulic valve lifters, regular camshaft, full-pressure lubrication, 409-cu.-in. displacement, 10.0:1 compression ratio, temperature-controlled fan.

400-HP TURBO-FIRE 409*—Delivers 425 ft.-lb. maximum torque. Available with manual shift transmissions only. 409-cu.-in. displacement, 11.0:1 compression ratio, large four-barrel aluminum carburetor, dual exhaust, oil-wetted element air cleaner, cast aluminum intake manifold, special camshaft with mechanical valve lifters, tough-surface crankshaft bearings and extra-strong pistons. Cylinder heads feature large valves and smooth ports. Automatic choke, full-flow oil filter.

425-HP TURBO-FIRE 409*—A modified edition of the 400-hp V8. 11.0:1 compression ratio, twin four-barrel carburetors, dual exhaust. Available with 3- and 4-Speed Synchro-Mesh transmissions only.

FOUR TRANSMISSIONS

STANDARD 3-SPEED SYNCHRO-MESH—Smooth, dependable, easy-shifting. Standard on all full-size Chevrolets. All-helical gear design with high torque capacity. Gear ratios matched to engine type.

OVERDRIVE*—Delivers top gas economy and reduces engine wear. 3-Speed Synchro-Mesh, plus 2-speed planetary Overdrive, engaged semi-automatically above approximately 30 mph.

4-SPEED SYNCHRO-MESH*—Aluminum case, all-helical gear design. All forward gears are fully synchronized. Choice of ratios with 400- and 425-hp 409-cu.-in. V8's. Central floor-mounted shift lever.

NEW POWERGLIDE*—For liquid-smooth and dependable automatic shifting. Two-speed three-element torque converter with hydraulically controlled planetary gears. Aluminum housing. Positive parking lock. Selector sequence Park-R-N-D-L.

1963 CHEVROLET POWER TEAMS

Standard Engines	3-Speed Synchro-Mesh	Overdrive*	4-Speed Synchro-Mesh*	Powerglide*
140-hp Turbo-Thrift 230	3.08:1 axle	3.70:1 axle		3.08:1 axle**
195-hp Turbo-Fire 283		3.70:1 axle		3.08:1 axle●
OPTIONAL V8's*				
250-hp Turbo-Fire 327		N.A.		3.08:1 axle
300-hp Turbo-Fire 327		N.A.		3.36:1 axle
340-hp Turbo-Fire 409		N.A.		3.36:1 axle
400-hp Turbo-Fire 409		N.A.		N.A.
425-hp Turbo-Fire 409		N.A.		N.A.

**3.55:1 in Station Wagons ; 3.36:1 in Impala Convert. ●3.36:1 in Station Wagon and all Impala models. N.A.—Not Available. †3.08:1 with 2.54:1 low transmission. *Optional at extra cost.

FUEL CAPACITY: Wagons, 19 gals ; all others, 20 gals. ELECTRICAL SYSTEM: 12-volt system, 54-plate battery (66-plate with 327- and 409-cu.-in. V8's). DIMENSIONS: Wheelbase, 119" Front and rear tread, 60.3" and 59.3". Overall: length, 210.4"; width, 79.0"; height—Sport Cpe. 54.5", Convert. and Sport Sed. 55.0", Wagons 56.0", others 55.5".

This would be a middling year for industry production. Calendar year sales for Chevrolet were down from 1963 but sales for Ford, Chrysler and most other models were up slightly. It was almost as if the market were catnapping before the staggering year to come.

The big news for the Chevrolet line this year was the introduction of the Super Sport as a series separate from the Impala. It was offered in Sport Coupe and Convertible form. Perhaps to emphasize its status as a separate series, the SS wore distinctive side trim. A bright piece ran along the upper edge of the concave, sculptured side. The patterned body trim accents and rear cove panel were silver. SS identification included the "SS" letters behind the "Impala" on the rear quarter panel and on the rear cove panel. The wheel covers carried the "SS" letters.

The interior of the SS was lavish. A new center console carried the Powerglide or four-speed transmission. Bucket seats were standard along with all vinyl upholstery. SS interior identification was carried on the console and the door panels. Special swirl-pattern interior trim was inserted on the instrument panel.

The SS shared with the Impala the triple taillight arrangement and the center chrome trim which ran from the hood to the rear deck and which distinguised the Impala from the Bel Air and Biscayne.

Length was 209.9" (210.8" station wagons) and width was 79.6". There were no changes to the engine line-up except for the deletion of the rarely seen RPO Z11 427 engine and the reduction of the standard 283 V-8 compression from 9.5:1 to 9.25:1. Two four-speed transmissions were now available with the 400- and 425-hp 409 engines: 2.56:1 low and 2.20:1 low.

Chevrolet production figures by body style were: 4d Sdn, 536,329; Spts Cpe, 442,292; Spts Sdn, 200,172; 4d Wgn, 192,827; 2d Sdn, 120,951; Convtbl, 81,897. Estimated production by series was: Biscayne, 173,900 (41,400 with V-8); Bel Air, 318,100 (180,300 with V-8); Impala, 889,600 (816,000 with V-8 and 185,325 SS's); station wagons, 192,800 (153,100 with V-8).

The least expensive Chevrolet this year was the Biscayne two-door sedan base priced at $2,471 (3,365 lbs.) and the most expensive was the Impala SS Convertible base priced at $3,196 (3,555 lbs.). The two-door Bel Air sedan was base priced at $2,573 (3,370 lbs.) and the Impala four-door sedan was base priced at $2,779 (3,460 lbs.).

Literature consisted of the full-line Chevrolet catalogue (pages 84-85) and an oversize standard Chevrolets catalogue (pages 83-82 and 86-87). The big Chevys were featured in a couple of interesing high performance ads this year, too (pages 80-81 and 88).

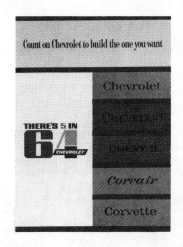

How Chevrolet makes roads feel smooth as the maps they're printed on

If you think this is going to be a lot of smooth talk about how luxuriously Chevrolet rides, you're right. But keep on reading. We've got all kinds of interesting facts and figures to back it up.

Those new roads on the map with the double red lines seem pretty nice in about any car.

But so do the old bumpy and hilly ones in a Chevrolet with Jet-smooth ride.

So what's Jet-smooth ride? It's not just a name for Chevrolet's suspension system, if that's what you think.

It's Chevrolet's luxury-car length, for one thing— 17½ feet from bumper to bumper—that makes bumps less noticeable.* And Chevrolet's luxury-car weight— from 3,375 to 4,045 lbs., depending on model and engine—that holds firmly to the road on curves.

It's over 700 sound quieters throughout the chassis and that big roomy Body by Fisher. Not to mention sound-absorbing wall-to-wall deep-twist carpeting that comes in every single Chevrolet model, even the lowest priced Biscaynes, wagons and all. And foam cushioning on Chevrolet's wide, comfortable seats, nearly

two inches thick on Impala models. (Sound sumptuous?)

It's Chevrolet's seven engines, each one precision-balanced for smoother running and longer life, ranging from the standard 140-hp Six all the way up to an extra-cost 425-hp V8. (You can see where the "jet" in Jet-smooth came from.) And Chevrolet's smooth-shifting transmissions, too.

And it's Chevrolet's Full Coil suspension—a big chrome-alloy steel coil spring and double-action shock absorber at each wheel. By the way, just to show you how fussy we are about the Chevrolet ride, we tailor the springs to the weight of the various models.

In short, Jet-smooth ride is really just about everything that makes Chevrolet an honest-to-goodness luxury car.

About the only thing that *doesn't* is the Chevrolet price. . . . Chevrolet Division of General Motors, Detroit, Michigan.

Chevrolet • Chevelle • Chevy II • Corvair • Corvette

CHEVROLET

THE GREAT HIGHWAY PERFORMERS

*You *could* get technical about it and say it's really Chevrolet's long 119-inch wheelbase (that's the distance between front and rear axles). But you know what we mean.

Chevrolet Impala Super Sport Coupe with bucket seats

GENERAL MOTORS *Futurama*
NEW YORK WORLD'S FAIR

Jet-smooth Luxury Chevrolet

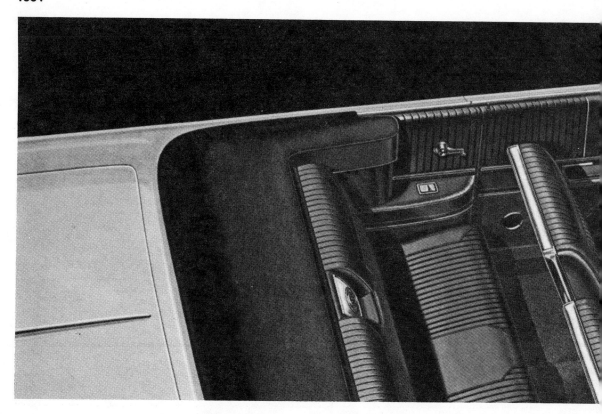

CHEVROLET INTERIORS

IMPALA SUPER SPORT—Luxury lovers, this interior's for you. New soft expanded vinyl in a pleated design covers most seat and door panel areas. And there's deep-twist carpeting underfoot. Extra-thick foam-cushioned seats will make SS the most sat-in car in the showroom. Especially the buckets up front. A smartly designed instrument panel puts all instruments and controls comfortably within easy eyesight and reach. Handsome center console houses 4-Speed* or Powerglide* shift levers along with a handy storage compartment (also a litter box in 3-Speed and Powerglide* models). Other goodies include bright SS identification trim, rear seat speaker grille and courtesy lights. Impala Super Sport has 8 color-keyed interiors including 3 exclusive two-tones. A car fit for any sporting jaunt.

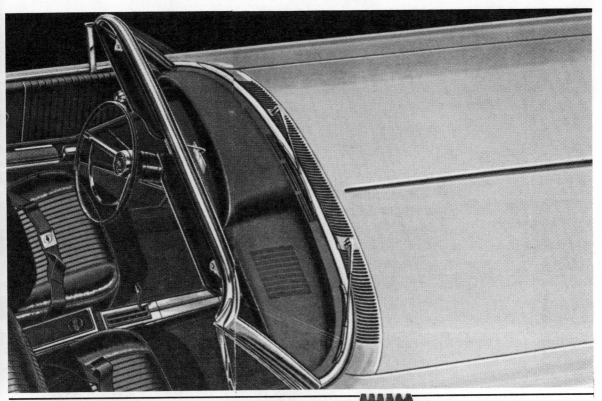

Impala Super Sport Coupe in Tuxedo Black

Impala Super Sport

Two sporty models in this fresh new series: Impala Super Sport Coupe and Convertible. Exclusive appointments in each with lavishly finished front bucket seats heading the list. Other neat SS touches: special wheel covers, body trim accents and nameplate. Beneath all this sporty beauty: Full Coil suspension for a Jet-smooth ride, easy-care features to save time and money. Fifteen color choices (six brand new) with Goldwood Yellow, a distinctive color shared by some Impalas. Standard engines: 140-hp Turbo-Thrift 230 six or 195-hp Turbo-Fire 283 V8. For extra spirit, five optional* engines including the popular 340-hp Turbo-Fire 409. Standard transmission: 3-Speed Synchro-Mesh. Powerglide* (featuring new "straight-line" shifting), Overdrive* or 4-Speed Synchro-Mesh* available.

*Optional at extra cost.

'64 Chevrolet . . . new looks in a great new Jet-smooth luxury lineup

Make no mistake about it. Chevrolet for '64 is luxury-size in everything but price. New series this year: Impala Super Sport. It joins Impala, Bel Air and Biscayne. Each brings new buying worth to the full-size field. In every model, exterior styling is freshly created, distinctively '64. Inside, rich fabrics and glove-soft vinyls tempt your eye and touch. Underway, the quiet comfort of a Jet-smooth ride. Plenty of room in an overall sedan length of 209.9 inches. Power? Sixteen engine-transmission combinations. Team up your choice for your own special brand of driving.

IMPALA SUPER SPORT COUPE IN DAYTONA BLUE

Impala Super Sport Interiors

Great for luxury lovers. Extra-thick foam cushioning in front buckets and full-width rear seat. Deep-twist carpeting underfoot. New soft expanded-vinyl treatment for seats and door panel areas. Bright-trimmed center console houses 4-Speed* or Powerglide* shift levers and handy storage compartment. Other niceties: bright SS identification trim, rear speaker grille and courtesy lights. Eight color-keyed interiors.

*Optional at extra cost.

NEW & IMPROVED TRANSMISSIONS

Frankly, we felt our transmission lineup was top quality last year. But we wanted to be sure our owners again have the absolute best. So this year, there's an improved 3-Speed Synchro-Mesh and a new 4-Speed Synchro-Mesh*. Powerglide* and Overdrive* will carry on as their smooth, efficient selves.

IMPROVED STANDARD 3- The big word on SPEED SYNCHRO-MESH Chevrolet's 3-Speed Synchro-Mesh this year is "quiet." Featuring an all-helical gear design with a high torque capacity, 3-Speed Synchro-Mesh is standard on all full-size Chevrolets. Gear ratios are, of course, matched to engine type for smooth, economical operation.

NEW 4-SPEED SYNCHRO-MESH*— Take an outstanding 4-Speed Synchro-Mesh transmission, do some rearranging and the result is an even better version. The all-helical gear design has an aluminum housing. As the name suggests, all forward gears are fully synchronized. And with the 400- or 425-hp 409 V8's*, there's a choice of gear ratios. Central floor-mounted shift lever for the sporting set.

RENOWNED AUTOMATIC POWERGLIDE*— Automatic Powerglide will be generating its share of excitement in '64. A two-speed three-element torque converter with hydraulically controlled planetary gears is contained in an aluminum housing. That's good for the power-to-weight ratio. The selector dial reads: Park (a positive parking lock)—R—N—D—L. All positions on SS floor-shift models fall in a straight line for easy gear selection.

EXTRA ECONOMICAL OVERDRIVE*— Ask the man on a limited gas budget about Overdrive. 3-Speed Synchro-Mesh works with a 2-speed planetary Overdrive to deliver top fuel economy and reduce engine wear. Overdrive is engaged semi-automatically when you exceed 30 mph, or thereabouts.

7 performance-wise ENGINES

Two fuel misers, the 140-hp Turbo-Thrift 230 six and the 195-hp Turbo-Fire 283 V8, qualify in the spirited category. Both thrive on regular gas. More ginger means the two 327-cu.-in. Turbo-Fire V8's*. And the mightiest of all are three ver-

sions of the 409 V8*. All Chevrolet engines feature valve-in-head design, aluminum pistons, positive-shift starter, positive crankcase ventilation and automatic choke. The 409 V8's* add sparkle to their exhilaration with chrome-plated rocker covers, air cleaner, oil dipstick and filler cap, and fuel lines.

STANDARD 140-HP TURBO-THRIFT 230— Economy, efficiency and spunk—words that really pinpoint Chevrolet's compactly designed 140-hp 6-cylinder power plant for 1964. Here's why. Thin-wall construction for cylinder head and block keeps weight down to a minimum. Modified-wedge combustion chambers and short stroke design yield an 8.5:1 compression ratio. Seven main bearings provide exceptional sturdiness. And full-pressure lubrication contributes to smooth operation. Other items: single-barrel carburetor, 230-cu.-in. displacement, oil-wetted air cleaner and full-flow oil filter.

STANDARD 195-HP TURBO-FIRE 283 V8— Chevrolet's 195-hp Turbo-Fire 283 has a camshaft that opens intake and exhaust valves wide to promote engine breathing and a liberal flow of fuel-air mixture to the combustion chambers. The fuel-air mixture is squeezed tightly by the compression ratio of 9.25:1. Additional assistance comes from a double-barrel carburetor, full-pressure lubrication system and a dry-element air cleaner.

250-HP AND 300-HP TURBO-FIRE 327*— Here's how to make two engines out of the same 327 cubic inches. First engine has a temperature-controlled fan, full-pressure lubrication system with full-flow oil filter, hydraulic valve lifters, a dry-element air cleaner, a four-barrel carburetor and dual exhausts. There's one goer with 250 horses and a 10.5:1 compression ratio. Now substitute a big aluminum-body 4-barrel carburetor, larger inlet valves and larger diameter dual exhaust system. The horsepower just jumped to 300 with the same compression ratio. Of course, you get a high power-to-weight ratio for efficiency and performance.

340-HP, 400-HP & 425-HP TURBO-FIRE 409*— Our favorite modern traffic goer is a 340-hp engine with high torque characteristics, single four-barrel carburetor, hydraulic valve lifters, regular camshaft, full-pressure lubrication, full-flow oil filter, closed positive-type engine ventilation, 10.0:1 compression ratio, temperature-controlled fan and full dual exhaust system. There's more performance yet in the 400-horse version. Large four-barrel aluminum carburetor, 11.0:1 compression, oil-wetted element air cleaner, cast aluminum intake manifold, special camshaft with mechanical valve lifters, tough-surface crankshaft bearings and extra-strong pistons. Cylinder heads feature large inlet valves and smooth ports. The 425-hp 409 is a further adaptation with twin four-barrel carburetors.

BODY BY FISHER
sets a standard in fine car quality

When it comes to quality construction in the Chevrolet body, Fisher Body craftsmanship welcomes comparison. The people at Fisher Body are masters who devote their undivided attention to details—construction details that assure you of a Chevrolet product you'll be proud to call your own for years to come.

CHEVROLET POWER TEAMS FOR 1964				
STANDARD ENGINES	**3-Speed Synchro-Mesh**	**Overdrive***	**4-Speed Synchro-Mesh***	**Powerglide***
140-hp Turbo-Thrift 230	3.08:1 axle**	3.70:1 axle	N.A.	3.08:1 axle**
195-hp Turbo-Fire 283	3.08:1 axle***	3.70:1 axle	N.A.	3.08:1 axle***
OPTIONAL V8's*				
250-hp Turbo-Fire 327	3.36:1 axle	N.A.	3.36:1 axle	3.08:1 axle
300-hp Turbo-Fire 327	3.36:1 axle	N.A.	3.36:1 axle	3.36:1 axle
340-hp Turbo-Fire 409	N.A.	N.A.	3.36:1 axle	3.36:1 axle
400-hp Turbo-Fire 409	N.A.	N.A.	3.36:1 axle	N.A.
425-hp Turbo-Fire 409	N.A.	N.A.	3.36:1 axle†	N.A.

**3.55:1 in Station Wagons; 3.36:1 in Convertibles. ***3.36:1 in Station Wagons and all Impala and Impala Super Sport models. N.A.—Not Available. †3.08:1 with 2.56:1 low transmission. *Optional at extra cost.

no high price on luxury here—just sport and sparkle...breeziness and breadth...and jet-smooth luxury!

if YOU LIKE PLAYING WITH BLOCKS, TRY THIS. With Chevrolet's Turbo-Fire 409 V8* block you can build to great heights. Say, 340 hp. 400 hp. Or, with the ingredients shown here, 425 hp. All three use the same block. Looks like the Rock of Gibraltar with 409 cubic inches of tunneling punched in it.

For the 425-hp 409 we add all those lovingly machined, cast and forged items above. Twin 4-barrel carburetors. Impact-extruded pistons. Forged steel connecting rods and five-main-bearing crankshaft. Cast alloy iron camshaft. And two heads fitted with lightweight valves. Mechanical valve lifters. Along with things we didn't show—header-type exhaust manifolds, dual exhausts, special clutch and heavy-duty radiator and suspension, among others. For the tamer 340- and 400-hp 409's, we use tamer bits and pieces here and there.

You can tuck a 425-hp Turbo-Fire 409 V8 into any '64 Chevrolet Biscayne, Bel Air, Impala or Impala Super Sport. And choose low gear ratios of 2.56:1 or 2.20:1 with the 4-speed all-synchro shift*. With the 2.20:1 gear ratio you can get 4.11:1 or 4.56:1 Positraction High Performance axle ratios*. Isn't playing with blocks fun?... Chevrolet Division of General Motors, Detroit, Michigan.

CHEVROLET

*Optional at extra cost

This year industry production would exceed 9,000,000 units and Chevrolet calendar year production would follow suit with total 1965 production of 2,587,490 units.

The radical redesign of 1965 was very well regarded at the time and has worn equally well since among commentators, critics and enthusiasts alike. The boxey look which had evolved during the previous years was gone and in its place a sleeker, more streamlined look was created. This effect was achieved in no small measure by the curved glass side windows. The redesign started from the chassis where the "X" frame (which had been in use since 1958) was replaced with the "Girder Guard" perimeter frame.

The SS returned as a separate series this year. It was visually separated from the rest of the Impalas by the removal of the rocker trim, "Super Sport" identification script behind the front wheel housing, "SS" nameplate on the front grille and on the right of the rear black insert trim band. Wheel caps contained "SS" red-filled letters.

Interior SS appointments continued the increasing trend of Impala luxury. All-vinyl upholstery covered the front bucket seats. The center console was available in two versions, depending on your choice of transmission. The instrument panel was new and, for once, contained more than just your textured, silver inset. This time the SS was standard with instrumentation which included oil, temperature and amp guages in the bezel left of the speedometer. The right bezel contained either a vacuum guage or a tachometer.

Among the many mid-year introductions this year, Chevrolet would add the Caprice option to the Impala series. The Caprice would differ from the "SS" version of the Impala in many ways. First, it was only available as a V-8. Second, it rested on a heavier frame and had special mountings and sound-deadening material. Third, it had special recalibrated shocks. The Caprice did retain visual identification with the "SS" as it carried the black-accented front grille and rear panel. It also carried unique Caprice features such as the "fluer-de-lis" on the rear roof, special body-sill moldings and, typically, the vinyl roof option. The Caprice option added around $200 to the price of the Impala.

The Impalas continued to carry the distinctive triple taillight arrangement. Bel Air and Biscayne were limited to Sedan and Station Wagon models.

The new body was extended to 213" in length (still on the 119" wheelbase) and 79.6" in width. The initial model introduction was greeted with sighs of disappointment in many areas. The motoring press and enthusiasts had been expecting to see the introduction of a major new engine. Instead, they saw the top of the line performance engine: the 400-hp 409. Good as that was, they were expecting more. They got more with the February 15, 1965, introduction of the 396 cu. in. V-8 in 325- or 425-hp form. The "Daytona Mystery Engine" was a mystery no more. Officially known as the Mark IV, this V-8 was to be known to the publicists as the "Turbo-Jet" V-8. This year the 325-hp version would be limited to Impala, Impala SS and Caprice models, although the 425-hp version was available on any model from a lowly Biscayne, up. With the introduction of this engine the Turbo Hydra-Matic transmission was also made available. There was also news on the six cylinder front. A new 250 cu. in. 150-hp I-6 was introduced with 9.5:1 compression and 1-bbl carburetion.

Body style production figures were: Spts Cpe, 558,459; 4d Sdn, 480,801; Spts Sdn, 252,048; 4d Wgn, 184,316; 2d Sdn, 99,188; Convtbl, 72,760. Estimated production by series: Biscayne, 145,300 (37,600 with V-8); Bel Air, 271,400 (163,600 with V-8); Impala, 803,400 (746,800 with V-8); Impala SS, 243,144 (239,500 with V-8 and 27,842 were Convertibles); station wagons, 184,400 (155,000 with V-8).

The least expensive Chevrolet (exluding station wagons) was the Biscayne two-door sedan with a base price of $2,419 (3,455 lbs.) and the most expensive was the Impala SS Convertible with a base ticket of $3,146 (3,645 lbs.). The Bel Air two-door sedan was base priced at $2,520 (3,460 lbs.) and the Impala four-door sedan was base priced at $2,722 (3,595 lbs.).

Literature this year considered of the full-line Chevrolet brochure (pages 92-93) and the standard-size Chevrolets brochure covering the Impala SS, Impala, Bel Air and Biscayne (pages 90-91 and 98-100). A nice series of high performance ads featuring the big Chevys also appeared (pages 94-97).

Impala Super Sport Convertible in Regal Red.

IMPALA SUPER SPORT

SPORTS NEW ELEGANCE WITH GUSTO

Distinctive grille has special SS nameplate.

Exclusive Super Sport wheel cover.

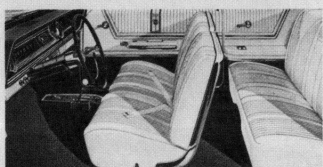
Impala Super Sport Coupe with all-vinyl front bucket seats in white.

Impala Super Sport Coupe in Evening Orchid.

Chevrolet is totally new for 1965. That's simple fact. And no series better reflects this total newness than Impala Super Sport. New hood contours, curved side glass and ground-hugging lines: Impala Super Sport really expresses the promise of innovations. The new Sweep-line roof of the Impala Super Sport Coupe headlines an automobile of style and distinction. And so does the profile of the SS Convertible. With Chevrolet's new Girder-Guard frame, Wide-Stance design, improved Full Coil suspension and adhesively bonded windshield, Impala Super Sport is *the* series for those who like their newness in sizable portions.

Inside, a new center console houses a rally-type electric clock capable of ticking off time between checkpoints or tourist attractions. Deep-twist carpeting complements the soft vinyl upholstery on sporty front bucket seats. And the full instrumentation (including a new built-in vacuum gauge) tells you the instrument panel is all business.

Just wait till you get Impala Super Sport on the road. Chevrolet's standard 140-hp Six or 195-hp V8 (depending on the model you choose) provides the spirit. If out-and-out gusto's your aim, there are four other V8s available, ranging from 250 hp to 400 hp. You can couple your engine with standard 3-Speed Synchro-Mesh or specify economical Overdrive, automatic Powerglide or 4-Speed Synchro-Mesh. Powerglide and 4-Speed have a console-mounted floor shift. The going's sportiest of all when you order features such as a tachometer, deluxe AM/FM pushbutton radio with FM stereo, Comfortilt steering wheel, Four-Season air conditioning, windshield-mounted compass and Positraction rear axle.

Make your 1965 Chevrolet exactly right for you with Chevrolet's extra-cost Options and Custom Features, some of which have been described and illustrated in this catalog. Pages 18 and 19 contain a detailed listing.

Curved side glass adds elegance to clean contours.

NEW FEATURES: Dynamically new body styling • Adhesively bonded windshield and rear window • Curved side window glass • Convertible tempered plate glass rear window • Fork-type door latches • Pop-up hood latch • Additional body mounts • Improved front and rear suspension • Girder-Guard frame • Wide-Stance tread • Improved camshaft for 6-cylinder engine • Oil-wetted paper-element air cleaner for V8s • One-piece drive shaft • Newly designed rear axle • Impala Super Sport dimensions: Wheelbase—119"; Front tread—62.5", rear tread—62.4", Overall length—213.0"; Overall width—79.6"; Overall height—sport coupe 54.1" and convertible 55.1".

1965 CHEVROLET POWER TEAMS				
STANDARD ENGINES	3-Speed Synchro-Mesh	4-Speed Synchro-Mesh	Power-glide	Over-drive
140-hp Turbo-Thrift 230 6-cylinder	●		●	●
195-hp Turbo-Fire 283 V8	●	●	●	●
EXTRA-COST OPTIONAL ENGINES				
250-hp Turbo-Fire 327 V8	●	●	●	
300-hp Turbo-Fire 327 V8	●	●	●	
340-hp Turbo-Fire 409 V8		●	●	
400-hp Turbo-Fire 409 V8		●		

5

Impala Super Sport Coupe in Crocus Yellow

'65 CHEVROLET

EXCITING NEW LOOK OF ELEGANCE

In a glance, total luxury and new styling—the most beautiful full-size Chevrolet yet built. In size, longer, lower, wider this year. New roof lines and curved side windows. New tempered glass rear window in convertible top. Interiors give you more comfort than you would expect. More shoulder, leg and foot room. Rich new upholsteries in fabrics and textured vinyls. New four-position ignition switch.

Underneath, a completely new chassis. New Girder-Guard frame, front and rear suspension, steering linkage, rear axle and Wide-Stance tread design—all adding to Chevrolet's luxurious, smooth ride, solid construction and easy-handling stability. A total of 16 power teams with engines ranging from an economical Six to a 400-hp V8.

A host of easy-care features to cut service, increase savings. A selection of 15 models in four series: Impala Super Sport, Impala, Bel Air and Biscayne. Price? Bound to keep Chevrolet the car most seen in '65.

IMPALA SUPER SPORT

All-around sport and splendor in Chevrolet's most luxurious series. Two big ways to go: Impala Super Sport Coupe and Convertible. Each with the distinction of plush front bucket seats, SS wheel covers, deep grille styling, body trim ornamentation and nameplate. New frameless curved side glass windows in both models. Sleek new Sweep-line roof in the Super Sport Coupe. On the road, more comfort from improved ride features. In standard engines, a quieter 140-hp Turbo-Thrift 230 Six or 195-hp Turbo-Fire 283 V8, depending on model choice. Specify greater gusto in four other engines, including the popular 340-hp Turbo-Fire 409. Standard transmission, 3-Speed Synchro-Mesh. You can also order Powerglide, featuring "straight-line" range selection, 4-Speed Synchro-Mesh or Overdrive.

Available for personalizing: new AM/FM radio with FM stereo; air conditioning; Comfortilt steering wheel; power steering, brakes, windows; Positraction rear axle.

IMPALA SUPER SPORT INTERIORS

Prestige touches in tasteful proportions. Part of the comfort: thick foam cushioning in front and rear seats, deep-twist carpeting, blended-air heater-defroster, high-level ventilation. For your convenience: center console housing rally-type clock with sweep second hand, 4-Speed or Powerglide shift levers and carpet-lined storage compartment with courtesy lamp. Bright-metal trimmed pedal pads, full instrumentation including vacuum gauge. Rear speaker grille, automatic interior lights and front seat belts. Luxury from rich textured vinyl seats and door panels, two-tone instrument panel with brushed metal trim. Choose from eight color-keyed interiors.

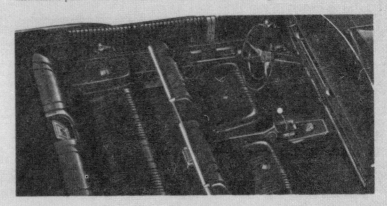

Include other items that satisfy your fancy for additional comfort and convenience. More Chevrolet Options and Custom Features, besides those described or shown here, are listed on the back of this catalog. At their moderate extra cost, you'll be happy you included them. 3

Two kinds of people fall in love with a Chevrolet Super Sport: emotional people and shrewd people

Find out below if you'll be one of them.

Now the emotional types are often first attracted to a Super Sport's rich all-vinyl interior (there's over 16 sq. yards of it).

To its deep foam-cushioned bucket seats—

And thick color-keyed carpeting that roams all over the floor, across the doors, up the cowl side panels and even into the floor console compartment.

They're impressed by the power they can have in a Super Sport—power that ranges from a responsive 140-hp Six to a brand-new Turbo-Jet V8.

By the wide variety of equipment offered—from a steering wheel that moves into seven different positions to a radio that plays in stereo.

And of course, by the little touches that make emotional people emotional people—curved side windows, a built-in vacuum gauge, an electric clock, brushed chrome trim, a solid tempered safety plate glass convertible rear window and so on.

As for the shrewd types, they of course know that a Super Sport is a full-size luxury car without a full-size luxury car price.

That a Chevrolet traditionally has maintained a high resale at trade-in time.

That it rides on a Jet-smooth easy street with its Full Coil suspension system. And keeps quiet about it all with 700 sound and shock deadeners.

That it is built to last—with things like a hefty single unit Body by Fisher and a 9-step acrylic lacquer exterior finish.

And that behind its good looks, there are some pretty sensible money-saving features like self-adjusting brakes with bonded linings, a battery-saving Delcotron generator and four inner steel fenders that protect the four outer steel fenders.

This all brings us back to you—and your particular love affair.

What will it be? Emotional? Shrewd? Or both?

Makes no difference.

As you'll soon find out at your dealer's—a Chevrolet-Super-Sport-kind-of-love is a many splendored thing.

Chevrolet Division of General Motors, Detroit, Michigan.

In the foreground, there sits an Impala Super Sport Convertible.
In the background, an Impala Super Sport Coupe.

1965

Irresistible model shown, '65 Chevrolet Impala Sport Coupe

Irresistible force—in an irresistible object
'65 CHEVROLET 409

Order a Chevrolet and ponder some irresistible choices, too.

Like our 409-cubic-inch V8 — which we'll tuck under any '65 Chevrolet at your request. (You could tuck it under Mount Rushmore and all that molten torque would make itself known.)

For '65, the 409 comes in two powerful forms: 340 hp (4-barrel carburetor, hydraulic lifters, 10.0:1 compression ratio) and

400 hp (aluminum 4-barrel, mechanical lifters, 11.0:1 compression ratio). Both have a larger, more durable clutch. And you can specify Delcotronic full-transistor ignition for either.

For the 409, we offer 409-style equipment: you can order 4-Speed Synchro-Mesh, Positraction, metallic brake linings and with the 340-hp version even special front and rear suspension.

The 409 makes the switch to the bigger, heftier '65 Chevrolet like it was born there. Leaving you with one problem—deciding which Chevrolet to put it in.

Don't you wish you had more problems like that?

Chevrolet Division of General Motors, Detroit, Michigan

MOTOR TREND/DECEMBER 1964 **7**

96

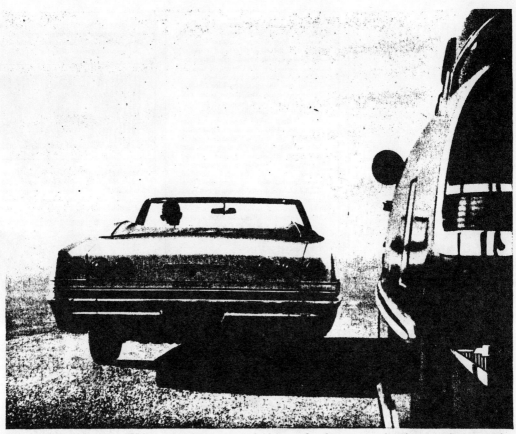

The 1955 Chevrolet V8 revised everyone's idea of what a production engine can do.
Here we go again, Charlie.

TURBO-JET 396 V8

Every once in a while, in engine design, something special happens.

Technological advancement, and pure research, and engineering skill all happen to reach the same peak at the same time. The result is an engine that stands head-and-shoulders above all the rest, that clearly exceeds what the public can ordinarily hope for.

That's what happened with the Chevrolet 265-cubic-inch V8 of 1955, which became the 283, and on which the 327 is based. Everyone knows about those great engines.

And that's what happened with this one. You're going to see a lot of it.

MAY 1965

The official name is Turbo-Jet 396 V8.

A new generation of engines begins right here.

396 cubic inches. 4.094 x 3.76 bore and stroke. 325 bhp at 4800 rpm, with 410 lb-ft of torque at 3200 rpm. From hydraulic valve lifters and one 4-bbl. carburetor. There's also a 425-horsepower version. (That's 1.073 hp per cubic inch in specific output.) Either is available in any Impala model.

This new power comes from very high volumetric efficiency, from a particularly advanced head design. Separately mounted rocker arms allow individually located valves,

inlet ports, exhaust ports and precisely right combustion chamber design for remarkably good breathing characteristics. The engine breathes well, reacts quickly, and will provide durability of the sort that people have come to expect from Chevrolet.

Just try one, and see how we've understated the case. Chevrolet Division of General Motors, Detroit, Michigan.

11

1965 QUALITY ENGINEERING HIGHLIGHTS

STANDARD ENGINES

(depending on the model you choose)

140-hp Turbo-Thrift 230. Chevrolet's standard 6-cylinder power plant has a new camshaft that provides increased valve train durability and quieter operation. Thin wall construction for cylinder head and block holds down weight. Short-stroke design and modified-wedge combustion chambers with 8.5:1 compression ratio. Seven main bearings, full-pressure lubrication, single-barrel carburetor, oil-wetted air cleaner and full-flow oil filter are among important features.

195-hp Turbo-Fire 283 V8. Chevrolet's 283-cu.-in. standard V8 features double-barrel carburetor, full-pressure lubrication system and a new oil-wetted paper-element air filter. The camshaft is contoured for lively V8 performance plus economy. This 195-hp engine also comes equipped with positive-shift starter, hydraulic valve lifters, automatic choke, and positive-type crankcase ventilation. Compression ratio is 9.25:1.

EXTRA-COST OPTIONAL ENGINES

250-hp and 300-hp Turbo-Fire 327. The 250-hp engine combines temperature-controlled fan, new cylinder heads, full-pressure lubrication system with full-flow oil filter, hydraulic valve lifters, oil-wetted paper-element air cleaner, a four-barrel carburetor and a new large-diameter single exhaust

system for outstanding performance. Compression ratio — 10.5:1. Substitute a big aluminum-body 4-barrel carburetor, larger intake manifold and a dual exhaust system ... you have a 300-hp version. The 250-hp and 300-hp Turbo-Fire 327 V8s can be specified on any Chevrolet model you choose.

340-hp and 400-hp Turbo-Fire 409. The 340-hp engine has high torque characteristics, single four-barrel carburetor, hydraulic valve lifters, full-pressure lubrication, full-flow oil filter, closed positive-type engine ventilation, 10.0:1 compression, temperature-controlled fan and full dual exhaust. A 400-hp plant is even brawnier with large four-barrel aluminum carburetor, 11.0:1 compression, oil-wetted paper-element air cleaner, cast aluminum intake manifold, special camshaft with mechanical valve lifters, tough-surface crankshaft bearings and extra-strong pistons. Cylinder heads feature large inlet valves and smooth ports. Both the 340-hp Turbo-Fire V8 and the 400-hp Turbo-Fire V8 are available on all Chevrolets.

TRANSMISSIONS

(See the power team charts on the individual model pages for exact transmission availability.)

3-Speed Synchro-Mesh. Standard on full-size Chevrolets (depending on engine), 3-Speed Synchro-Mesh has an all-helical gear design with a high torque capacity. Gear ratios are matched to engine.

4-Speed Synchro-Mesh. An all-helical gear design has an aluminum housing. Central floor-mounted shift lever with all forward gears fully synchronized. 400-hp 409 V8 fans get a choice of gear ratios. 4-Speed Synchro-Mesh is available with Chevrolet V8s.

Automatic Powerglide. Powerglide gets its smoothness from a three-element torque converter with hydraulically controlled two-speed planetary gears in an aluminum housing. Selector indicator reads: Park (a positive parking lock) — R — N — D — L. Models with floor-mounted shift feature straight-line gear selection.

Economical Overdrive. Overdrive is engaged semi-automatically at approximately 30 mph. 3-Speed Synchro-Mesh works with a 2-speed planetary gear unit for fuel economy and to reduce engine wear.

BODY BY FISHER

The quality construction of Chevrolet's 1965 body comes from Body by Fisher craftsmanship. Unisteel design means that roof, sides, floor and other body parts are solidly welded together to form a single unit. This unit is sealed, insulated and attached with extra-large (17.5% thicker than ever) rubber

mountings. A high-level ventilation system which provides air through special inlets high on the cowl complements Chevrolet's blended-air heater and defroster.

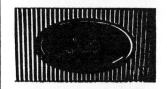

Magic-Mirror Finish. Magic-Mirror acrylic lacquer finish helps protect any one of 15 hues (13 new) and nine two-tones against chipping, sun-fading and the corrosive effects of salt and road tar.

Fork-Type Door Latches. Chevrolet's '65 door latches were engineered with a new fork-type design. An end cap on the latch bolt helps prevent lateral door movement. New Ignition Switch. '65 Chevrolet has a new four-position ignition switch (Accessory, Off, On, Start) that prevents key removal without locking the ignition.

EASY-CARE FEATURES

Flush-and-Dry Rocker Panels. Water entering the cowl inlet ventilation system is directed to the rocker panels where it flushes dirt and dust out through built-in drains. Incoming air follows the same channels and dries panel interiors.
Inner Fenders. Inner front and rear fenders do an excellent job of fending off water, mud and road salt, protect outer panels.
Self-Adjusting Safety-Master Brakes. Chevrolet's 11-inch hydraulic brakes have 198.4 sq. in. of wheel surface and large cylinders. Bonded linings provide long life, and venting through wheel slots reduces the possibility of brake fade. Apply pressure to the brake pedal when backing up and the brakes adjust themselves automatically.

Extended-Life Exhaust System. Liberal use of aluminizing and/or stainless steel, plus heavy gauge tailpipes, means fewer replacements, more satisfactory service and miles of quiet full-power motoring.

Delcotron Generator. The self-contained, high-capacity Delcotron is extremely durable because there's no commutator to wear out. At low engine speeds, Chevrolet's Delcotron generator helps out with extra electrical output to save on battery wear. The 1965 Chevrolets have a 54-plate battery (66-plate with 327- and 409-cu.-in. V8s) and a 12-volt electrical system.

CHASSIS

New Girder-Guard Frame. An all-welded steel unit features full-length side rails joined laterally by four crossmembers. Torque-box construction of side rails between passenger and engine compartments prevents high stress concentrations in this area.

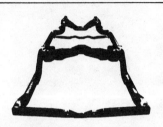

Ball-Race Steering. The new rear-mounted linkage for Chevrolet's '65 Ball-Race steering provides smooth, positive control. The overall ratio with standard steering is 28.3:1; power steering is 19.4:1.

Wheels and Tires. All full-size Chevrolets for 1965 have 14-inch wheels. Blackwall 7.35 x 14 tubeless tires are standard, except on the Convertibles (7.75 x 14) and all Station Wagons (8.25 x 14).

Full Coil Suspension. New coil spring independent suspension up front and link-type coil rear suspension handle a large portion of the 1965 Chevrolet ride. Rear suspension linkage, built around a new rear axle design, is tailored to model and engine to provide better stability, maneuverability, and more level cornering, acceleration and braking.

Clutch. Chevrolet's '65 clutch has a single dry disc with two facings and a release bearing with sealed-in lubricant. Actual size is determined by engine choice. All engines call for a diaphragm spring-type unit; optional, extra-cost V8s feature centrifugal assistance.

OPTIONS AND CUSTOM FEATURES AVAILABLE AT EXTRA COST*

Engines. 250-hp Turbo-Fire 327 V8 • 300-hp Turbo-Fire 327 V8 • 340-hp Turbo-Fire 409 V8 • 400-hp Turbo-Fire 409 V8
Transmissions. 4-Speed Synchro-Mesh • Powerglide • Overdrive
All-Transistorized AM/FM Radio with FM Stereo. Deluxe 5-pushbutton model that features automatic frequency control, straight-line tuning and static-free FM reception. Four speakers, two front and two rear. Pushbutton AM and AM/FM, and manual AM models are also available. A rear-seat speaker is available with both pushbutton versions. All Chevrolet radios are acoustically tailored to Chevrolet interiors.

Positraction Rear Axle. Ice, sand or snow, if one wheel can get a grip on the road, Positraction lets you go. Available with all Chevrolet power teams.
Power Steering. Extra-easy power steering with a hydraulic assist incorporated in the steering gear takes up to 90% of the effort out of cornering and parking.

Power Windows. One master control beside the driver's seat operates all windows, while a separate control at each window allows each passenger to adjust his own window height. Power windows can be purchased on all Impala SS, Impala and Bel Air models.
Power Brakes. A boon to highway or city driving, power brakes require approximately ⅓ less pedal pressure for safe, efficient stops.
Four-Season Air Conditioning. Predict your own driving weather with Four-Season air conditioning. Air flow has been increased by about 10%, and a larger capacity receiver reduces refrigerant recharge time. In addition, new slide controls permit fast, easy regulation of humidity and temperature all year long.

Comfortilt Steering Wheel. Seven different positions to suit any driver. Comfortilt is available on all '65 models equipped with 4-Speed Synchro-Mesh or Powerglide.

6-Way Flexomatic Power Seat. Adjusts fore and aft, up or down, and tilts forward or back for individual comfort.

2-Speed Electric Windshield Wipers. Optional 2-speed electric windshield wipers give you two constant speeds whether you accelerate or apply the brakes. Parallel action eliminates center blind spots.
Additional Extra-Cost Equipment. Deluxe color-matched seat belts with retractors. Black vinyl top for Impala Sport Sedan and Sport Coupe and Impala SS Coupe. Black all-vinyl upholstery for Impala Sport Sedan and Sport Coupe and Impala SS Coupe. Sweep second hand electric clock. Clear vinyl and tinted translucent full-width floor mats. Soft-Ray tinted glass. Tri-Volume horn. Windshield-mounted auto compass. Remote-operated, fender-mounted spot lamp. Car-to-trailer electrical wiring harness. Wheels with 6-inch rims. Vented wheel covers. Special front springs. Special suspension. Simulated wire wheel covers. Superlift air-adjustable shock absorbers. Load-compensating automatic level control. Dual exhaust system for the 250-hp Turbo-Fire 327 V8. Heavy-duty clutch. Temperature-controlled fan. Heavy-duty radiator. Heavy-duty sintered-metallic brake linings. Padded instrument panel. Sports-styled steering wheel. Extra-heavy foam-cushioned front seat. Two-tone finish. Guards for front and rear bumper. Comfort and Convenience Equipment. Whitewall tires. Oversized and special tires. Heavy-duty Delcotron generators. Heavy-duty battery. 3.36:1 and 3.55:1 ratio rear axles. Tachometer. Oil-bath air cleaner and closed positive-type crankcase ventilation for 6-cylinder engine. Power-operated station wagon tailgate window. Key lock for station wagon hidden stowage area. Station wagon split second seat. Five-stanchion station wagon roof luggage carrier. Special police or taxicab equipment. Full line of Custom Feature Accessories.

*Check your Chevrolet dealer for model application and availability with other equipment 19

8   Impala Convertible with red interior.

After the heady, record setting sales year in 1965, it was not surprising that 1966 would be a year of mild retrenchment. Chevrolet was no different from the rest with calendar year sales dropping to 2,202,806.

The Impala SS was again available in Sport Coupe and Covertible form. Exterior trim was virtually identical to the Impala which was only mildly face-lifted from the 1965 redesign (side crease molding trim was apparently included to minimize the problems of paint chipping encountered by the 1965 owners in parking lot duels with unneighborly door edges). The SS was identifiable only by the "Super Sport" script which replaced the Impala emblem behind the front wheel house, the SS emblem on the grille and rear and was inset in the tri-blade wheel caps. The SS, like the rest of the Impala line, barely retained its now-traditional triple taillights. The new lights were rectangular and, like Gaul, were all divided into three parts (in this case by thin chrome strips).

The SS was rapidly losing its unique identity and was becoming little more than a cosmetic package to the Impala. Interior differences between an SS and an Impala were slim. The attractive Strato-bucket seats with center console were standard. The center console was a new design. The SS emblem was carried on the glove box door. Gone, however, was the performance instrument cluster as standard equipment. A tachometer was available as an option.

The Caprice emerged as this year's big model news. A prior mid-model-year introduction, the Caprice clearly claimed title to the distinction of being Chevrolet's luxury leader. The Impala would wear that title no more. The Caprice was offered in Custom Coupe or Custom Sedan form. Two station wagon versions were also available. The rocker panel molding was bolder than that offered on the Impala and taillights were of one piece divided by thin horizontal bars.

The Caprice did include as part of the Custom Coupe sport interior an instrument gauge package on the center console. The standard Caprice came with an extremely high grade of interior trim including deep padded vinyl seats.

The Bel Air and Biscayne were available in two and four door sedans and station wagons.

Length was extended to 213.2" (212.4" on station wagons) and width was 79.6". The new engine this year was the 427 based on the Mark IV 396 introduced in mid-model year 1965. This new engine was top-rated at 425-hp with extra solid lifters, four bolt block and 4-bbl carburetor with 11:1 compression. An SS, following tradition, could be ordered with a Turbo-Thrift 250 Six but the Caprice was only available with a V-8. All engines were available on Bel Air and Biscayne. Cars equipped with the 427 or 396 V-8 were identified by a black bar with the engine designation which was pierced by the crossed flag vee. The 327 engine was identified by the "327" resting on the crossed flag vee.

Model year production was: Biscayne 122,400 (39,200 with V-8); Bel Air, 236,600 (164,500 with V-8); Impala, 654,900 (621,800 with V-8); Impala SS, 119,314 (118,400 with V-8 and 15,872 Convertibles); Caprice, 181,000. Station wagon production figures are not separately available.

The least expensive Chevrolet (excluding station wagons) was the Biscayne two-door sedan at $2,482 (3,445 lbs.) and the most expensive was the Impala SS Convertible at $3,199 (3,630 lbs.). The Bel Air two-door sedan was base priced at $2,584 (3,445 lbs.) and the Impala four-door sedan was base priced at $2,783 (3,565 lbs.). The Caprice and Impala hardtop sedans were base priced at $3,063 (3,675 lbs.) and $2,852 (3,650 lbs.) respectively.

Literature this year consisted of a beautiful big Chevrolets catalogue (page 106) as well as a full-line piece (page 102). There was also a mailer issued entitled "Chevrolet Brings You The News Via The Huntley-Brinkley Report" which illustrated the Impala SS (page 103) and a couple of nice big Chevys high performance ads (pages 104-105).

Impala Convertible in Artesian Turquoise.

Impala 3-Seat Station Wagon in Marina Blue.

1966 Chevrolet

IMPALA SUPER SPORT AND IMPALA

Two luxurious series, Impala Super Sport and Impala, both with a convertible and sweepline-styled sport coupe. Plus a hardtop sport sedan, 4-door sedan, 2- and 3-seat wagons in the Impala series. Jet-smooth ride, naturally, including special quiet-ride chassis components in hardtops. Lustrous metal highlights along the sides and around wheel openings add sparkle. Interiors are rich. Strato-bucket front seats are standard in Super Sports. All seats are foam cushioned. Armrests with fingertip door releases built in. Electric clock with sweep second hand. Parking brake warning light. Back-up lights. Even automatic illumination when you open front doors, the glove compartment or the spacious trunk. Up to eight interior hues, 15 Magic-Mirror exterior colors. Order an Impala with Turbo Hydra-Matic transmission . . . the ultimate in automatic driving.

Impala Super Sport Coupe in Regal Red.

4

Chevrolet Impala Super Sport Coupe in Lemonwood Yellow

As for the full-size Chevrolet, there's more of a choice than ever in hardtops. This one is an Impala Super Sport Coupe. You might prefer the luxury of a Caprice Custom Coupe or Sedan with hardtop styling; or possibly the pleasant surroundings of an Impala Sport Coupe or Sport Sedan. It's an-odds-on favorite that your Chevrolet dealer has one that's harnessed and ready for you.

The big news isn't the gauges . . .
it's what the gauges connect to!

The real news about Impala is the 427-cu.-in. Turbo-Jet V8 you can put on the other side of the firewall to make the needles quiver. The street version generates 390 hp and 415 lbs.-ft. of torque on hydraulic lifters. A special-purpose edition turns out 425 hp and the same amount of torque on solid (ah, what sounds!) lifters.

Both engines are of the same unique design that inspired our successful Turbo-Jet 396, which is now rated at 325 hp. Intake and exhaust ports feed directly to the combustion chambers with little interference from valves and pushrods. As a result, the Turbo-Jets breathe in a manner that makes ordinary engines feel short-winded

— even downright asthmatic.

As for the gauges — they're important, too. In fact, we're confident that the man who knows what's happening inside the engine compartment is a safer, more alert driver. Drive as only you know how — and who knows? — maybe the less knowledgeable drivers will get the message.

'66 IMPALA by CHEVROLET

Chevrolet Division of General Motors, Detroit, Michigan.

TURBO-JET 427 V8

do not tease

'66 Chevrolet Impala SS Coupe—new standard safety package includes outside rearview mirror. Always check it before passing.

Poke the gas pedal of this new Chevrolet Turbo-Jet V8 and you get action. A full 427 cubic inches of it.

Its advanced design, with tilted valves and deep-breathing ports, sees to that.

Say you choose to cage it in that bucket-seated Impala SS above (it's available in 18 other Chevrolets, too). You can order it with hydraulic lifters and an output of 390 hp. Or you can order a version with special-performance camshaft, solid lifters—and 425 hp.

Either way, you get higher rate front and rear springs, heavy-duty shocks all around and 8.25 x 14 tires as part of the Turbo-Jet 427 package.

Sound like a lot of machine? As any road will show you, it's the most.

Quality engineering adds to Chevrolet worth

ENGINES

Chevrolet's engine roster for '66 boasts new power plants for a wide range of performance requirements. You can have a standard Six or a V8, depending on the model you select; or you can order extra-cost V8s with horsepower up to 425. All Chevrolet engines have these important engine characteristics: high-strength precision castings; efficient overhead valves, wedge-shaped combustion chambers and short inlet and exhaust ports; controlled pressure lubrication system with full-flow filter; pressurized cooling system and high-capacity water pump; and individually tailored fuel induction system.

STANDARD ENGINES (Depending on model selected.)

150-hp Turbo-Thrift 250 Six. This new standard engine has thin wall construction to hold down weight. Efficiency and economy are derived from a single-barrel carburetor, automatic choke, economy-contoured camshaft, and short-stroke design. Seven main bearings and extra crankshaft counterweights assure exceptional smoothness and durability. Compression ratio — 8.5:1.

195-hp Turbo-Fire 283 V8. Significant features include quality-engineered two-barrel carburetor, automatic choke, oil-wetted paper-element air filter, hydraulic valve lifters, positive-shift starter and positive-type engine ventilation. The camshaft is contoured to supply V8 efficiency with economical operation. Compression ratio is 9.25:1.

EXTRA-COST OPTIONAL ENGINES

220-hp Turbo-Fire 283 V8. This version of the standard V8 offers smooth, reliable operation. It incorporates a 4-barrel carburetor with automatic choke, dual exhaust system with resonators, general-performance camshaft and hydraulic valve lifters. Compression ratio—9.25:1.

275-hp Turbo-Fire 327 V8. A new version of the popular Turbo-Fire 327, this engine has a four-barrel carburetor and high compression ratio of 10.5:1. Other features: new automatic choke control, hydraulic valve lifters, general-performance camshaft and large-diameter single exhaust system with resonator. This engine can be ordered for all new Chevrolets.

325-hp Turbo-Jet 396 V8. Available on all full-size Chevrolets, this durable V8 features an advanced design —valves, valve ports and combustion chambers are engineered for maximum volumetric efficiency. Its extra efficiency at all engine speeds contributes to an overall economy that's excellent for an engine rated at 325 horsepower. Key components include four-barrel carburetor with automatic choke, hydraulic valve lifters and single exhaust system with resonator. Compression ratio—10.25:1.

390-hp Turbo-Jet 427 V8. This engine incorporates the basic design principles of the Turbo-Jet 396 and is available in two versions for all full-size Chevrolet '66 models. A four-barrel carburetor, new automatic choke, special camshaft and hydraulic lifters plus a dual exhaust system with resonators are marks of the 390-hp edition. Compression ratio is 10.25:1.

425-hp Turbo-Jet 427 V8. This special version of the Turbo-Jet 427 has larger four-barrel carburetor, special camshaft, mechanical valve lifters, dual exhaust system and special air cleaner. Plus special components like high-strength pistons, temperature-controlled fan, extra-durable crankshaft, double-belt water pump and fan drive. Compression ratio is 11:1. This 425-hp V8 can be specified for all full-size Chevrolets.

TRANSMISSIONS

Chevrolet for '66 has a wide selection of transmissions — from shift-for-yourself manuals to effortless automatics. See the power team chart on this page for availability of specific transmissions with the various engines.

3-Speed Fully Synchronized. The new standard manual transmission (depending on engine) for full-size Chevrolets offers full synchronization of all forward gears for smoother shifting into first, second or third, when downshifting or accelerating. Shift lever is mounted on the steering column. Durable, dependable and economical, this transmission has wide helical gears, large synchronizers and high-capacity front and rear ball bearings. A special 3-Speed fully synchronized transmission is available for the 396 and 427 Turbo-Jet engines.

4-Speed Fully Synchronized. Manually controlled by a floor-mounted gearshift lever, this responsive quick-shifting transmission incorporates an all-helical gear design, fully synchronized forward gears and an aluminum housing. 4-Speed can be ordered with any Chevrolet V8. A close-ratio version and a heavy-duty model are available for the 425-hp Turbo-Jet.

Automatic Powerglide. Powerglide's three-element torque converter and hydraulically controlled two-speed planetary gears combine to produce smooth, swift operation. For quick passing action, an accelerator-actuated automatic mechanism downshifts into low range. Selector sequence reads Park-R-N-D-L for positive Parking lock-Reverse-Neutral-Drive-Low. Those models with the floor-mounted lever provide straight-line range selections. Powerglide is available with six-cylinder models and most V8s.

Automatic Turbo Hydra-Matic. Superior performance and quiet cruising characterize Chevrolet's newest transmission. A three-element torque converter with a compound three-speed planetary gearset design, Turbo Hydra-Matic shifts automatically through three forward speed ranges. It can be downshifted at speeds below 70 mph for quicker passing or to assist braking. Six-position selector is identified: Park-R-N-D-L2-L1 for positive Parking lock-Reverse-Neutral-Drive-Low 2 (for heavy stop-and-go traffic situations)-Low 1 (for ascending or descending steep grades). Turbo Hydra-Matic can be ordered for the 325-hp Turbo-Jet 396 and 390-hp Turbo-Jet 427.

Economical Overdrive. Combines 3-Speed fully synchronized transmission with standard Six or V8 or 220-hp V8 to lower engine speeds, reducing engine wear and fuel consumption. Overdrive is semi-automatically activated at about 30 mph by a switch on the instrument panel.

Clutch. Chevrolet clutches are of single dry disc design and include a release bearing with a sealed-in lubricant and light alloy aluminum housing. Clutch disc sizes and spring pressures are matched to individual engine torques for smooth shifting and long life. Standard engines utilize a diaphragm spring-type unit; optional, extra-cost V8s include clutches that feature centrifugal assistance.

SPECIFICATIONS

Wheelbase	119.0"
Width, overall	79.6"
Length, overall	
Station wagons	212.4"
Other models	213.2"
Tread	
Station wagons	front: 63.5" ..... rear: 63.4"
Other models	front: 62.5" ..... rear: 62.4"
Height, loaded	
Sedans	55.4"
Hardtop sedans	54.5"
Hardtop coupes	54.4"
Convertibles	55.3"
Station wagons	56.7"
Interior room, 4-door sedans	
Torso room	front: 39.1" ..... rear: 37.8"
Leg room	front: 42.2" ..... rear: 39.5"
Hip room	front: 63.9" ..... rear: 62.9"
Shoulder room	front: 62.3" ..... rear: 61.3"
Entrance height	front: 30.4" ..... rear: 29.9"
Luggage compartment volume (cu. ft.)	
Total	28.7
Usable (Sedans)	17.8
Station wagon cargo volume (cu. ft.)	
2-seat	106.1
3-seat	101.3
Turning diameter (feet)	
Curb-to-curb	40.8
Wall-to-wall	44.1
Steering ratio, overall	
Standard	28.3:1
Power	19.4:1

CHEVROLET POWER TEAM CHART FOR 1966

STANDARD ENGINES	STANDARD 3-SPEED FULLY SYNCHRONIZED	EXTRA-COST OPTIONAL TRANSMISSIONS			
		OVERDRIVE	4-SPEED FULLY SYNCHRONIZED	POWERGLIDE	TURBO HYDRA-MATIC
150-hp Turbo-Thrift 250 Six†	•	•		•	
195-hp Turbo-Fire 283 V8	•	•		•	
EXTRA-COST OPTIONAL ENGINES					
220-hp Turbo-Fire 283 V8	•	•	•	•	
275-hp Turbo-Fire 327 V8	•		•	•	
325-hp Turbo-Jet 396 V8	▲		•	•	•
390-hp Turbo-Jet 427 V8	▲		•		•
425-hp Turbo-Jet 427 V8	▲		•		

†Not offered for Caprice models. ▲ Special 3-Speed fully synchronized transmission, available as an extra-cost Option.

Industry sales slipped significantly from the previous highs and Chevrolet's sales were no exception. Calendar year sales peaked at 1,900,049, almost 600,000 units below 1965.

The Impala SS, like the rest of the Chevrolet line, was mildly restyled for 1967. With Caprice receiving all the attention as the luxury Chevrolet and the hot Chevelle duking it out with the GTO and Mustang in the performance market, it was increasingly obvious that there was little room in the Chevrolet stable for an Impala SS with true performance characteristics. This year there was little to visually distinguish the SS from an ordinary Impala Sport Coupe or Convertible other than the black-accented lower body sill and fender bright moldings which were substituted for the Impala body trim. Traditional grille, front fender and rear deck identification was carried. Special SS wheelcovers were still available but they were just the ordinary Impala issued covers gussied up.

In a departure from SS tradition, and in addition to the Strato-bucket front seats, bench seats with arm rests, called Strato-back bench seats, were offered. Upholstery was all-vinyl and there was an SS emblem on the glove box with traditional SS bright metal interior trim on the Coupe. A gauge package with tachometer was optionally available.

As the SS was increasingly becoming little more than an Impala trim option, an attempt at continuing performance in the Impala line was made with the SS 427 option on the SS. It could be had with the Impala SS trim plus a domed hood with simulated brushed-chrome air intake grille. It carried special exterior identification in the form of grille and rear deck emblems and a special "427" V-flagged emblem on the front fender. Interesting, if uncommon, "eyebrow" special accent stripes along the upper body molding were available. Wheels were 14x6 with thin red-stripe (or optional white) wide oval nylon tires. This performance option was, of course, built around the 427 V-8 385-hp engine, special springs and shock absorber, heavy-duty front stabilizer bar and heavy-duty suspension bushings. The engine was equipped with chromed air cleaner, valve rocker covers, oil filler and engine breather caps.

The Caprice continued to be the luxury model with a higher grade of interior appointments. Caprice side trim was carried on the lower body line

and backup lights were located in the rear bumper, rather than as part of the traditional Impala triple taillight arrangement.

The Bel Air and Biscayne were offered in two- and four-door models.

Length was 213.2" (212.4" station wagons) and width was 79.9". Engine availability was decreased this year. Top horsepower was rated at 385 on the 427 V-8. Only four V-8 options were available: the standard 195-hp 283; 275-hp 327 with 4-bbl; 325-hp 396; and the 385-hp 427. The 396 and 427 engines required either four-speed transmission or the heavy-duty optional three-speed or Turbo Hydra-Matic. Rear axle rations for these engines included with the three- or four-speed were the standard 3.31:1, an "economy" 3.07:1, a "performance" 3.55:1 or a "special" 3.73:1. For the first time, front disc brakes with special 15" Rally wheels were offered. Special rear air shocks with automatic level control were also first available this year.

Model year production was 1,201,700 units of which 92,800 were Biscayne (38,600 with V-8); 179,700 were Bel Air (138,200 with V-8); 575,600 were Impalas (556,800 with V-8); 76,055 were Impala SS (400 with the 250 Six, 2,124 with the SS 427 option and 9,545 Convertibles); 124,500 were Caprice; and 155,100 were wagons (140,700 with V-8).

The least expensive Chevrolet (excluding station wagons) was the two-door Biscayne sedan with a base price of $2,547 (3,465 lbs.) and the most expensive was the Impala SS Convertible with a base price of $3,254 (3,650 lbs.). The Bel Air two-door sedan carried a base tag of $2,647 (3,470 lbs.) and the four-door Impala sedan carried one of $2,828 (3,575 lbs.). The Caprice and Impala hardtop coupes had base prices of $3,078 (3,605 lbs.) and $2,845 (3,590 lbs.), respectively.

Literature this year was plentiful. The big Chevys had their own 32-page catalogue that was among the more elaborate produced during this period (pages 108-111 and 116). There was also the large "The '67 Super Sports by Chevrolet" folder (page 112) which included a full spread on the SS 427. An interesting 24-page piece for the family set was issued on towing with the Chevrolets. Finally, a small folder was issued suggesting prospects "Meet the Performance Champs" (page 113). There was an interesting SS 427 ad, as well (pages 114-115).

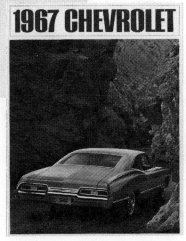

1967 CHEVROLET

The '67 Super Sports by Chevrolet

SPORTS MODELS:

Impala SS Coupe

As you can see, "SS" doesn't mean steamship (though it does leave plenty of admirers in its wake). The "SS" stands for Super Sport, a designation implying street rather than fleet. Try it on a piece of pavement and you'll see what we mean.

You'll probably want to send up a few flags yourself when you take in this low, sleek profile . . . exclusive new SS grille with distinctive black bars . . . new sports-styled wheel covers . . . special SS identification . . . black-accented chrome molding along the body sill and lower rear quarter.

In the control center, slim all-vinyl Strato-bucket front seats are standard or you can order a Strato-back front seat. With buckets, there's a center console with ashtray and lighted carpet-lined stowage compartment tossed in for good measure.

A special identification/performance package can be specified on Super Sport models when you order the 427-cu.-in. Turbo-Jet V8 with 385 horses. You get a domed hood with special brushed-chrome center ornaments, "SS 427" emblems on grille, fenders and deck lid, red stripe tires (white also available), 14" x 6" wheels, special springs and shocks, large-diameter front stabilizer bar and heavy-duty suspension bushings. Front wheel disc brakes and special body accent stripes are also available with the SS 427 package.

If you're a real stickler about what's going on under the hood, order the special instrumentation with tachometer and temperature, oil pressure and electrical gauges.

To build an Impala Super Sport just the way you want, notice the extra-cost Options and Custom Features shown or mentioned in this catalog and detailed on pages 29-31.

Special trim included with SS 427 package you can order.

Impala Super Sport interior in bright blue.

Shown on these pages: Impala Super Sport Coupe in Marina Blue.

Shown on these pages: Impala Super Sport Convertible in Bolero Red.

Impala Super Sport Convertible interior in red.

Data at a glance—the purpose behind the Impala SS instrument panel.

SPORTS MODELS:

Impala SS Convertible

Two Chevrolets are tagged with "Super." This is the one where you instinctively sit taller. Maybe because you can drop the top whenever the urge comes on. Or because you're always looked at with a trace of envy.

Seems as if those new lean-muscled looks really draw out spectators. Of course, the engine you swing with has a lot to do with confidence building. There are three extra-cost V8s you can specify with the SS convertible—a 275-hp Turbo-Fire 327, a 325-hp Turbo-Jet 396 and a 385-hp Turbo-Jet 427. The basic gearbox is a fully synchronized 3-Speed. You can slip it into first without stopping or fear of scrambling the works. You might prefer, however, to try your hand on the fully synchronized 4-Speed you can order. Or, depending on engine selected, Chevrolet's Turbo Hydra-Matic self-shifter or renowned Powerglide automatic.

Other performance-oriented equipment you can order are sintered-metallic brake linings, Positraction rear end in a number of axle ratios, special suspension. Don't forget the SS 427 equipment you can order with the 427-cu.-in. Turbo-Jet V8.

There are a number of other extra-cost Options and Custom Features shown or described in this catalog. A listing is on pages 29-31.

Chevrolet SS 427 Sport Coupe in Marina Blue.
(Convertible also available.)

Chevrolet SS 427

Mechanical features

385-hp Turbo-Jet 427 V8 engine (see chart at right for specs). Famed "porcupine" heads have individually ported inlet and exhaust passages. Low-restriction inlet runner shape and design. Angled valves for optimum gas flow. Inlet valves 2.065" diameter, exhaust valves 1.72" diameter. Valve lift .4614" inlet, .4800" exhaust. Inlet valves open 56° BTC, close 114° ABC, have 350° duration. Exhaust valves open 110° BBC, close 62° ATC, have 352° duration. Extra-thick bulkheads above each crankshaft bearing and wide-base main bearing caps for more rigid crankshaft clamping. High-strength castings. Special suspension components with SS 427.

Transmissions

Special 3-Speed fully synchronized. Extra-cost. Heavy-duty design features 2.41:1 first, 1.57:1 second, 1.00:1 third. 2.41:1 reverse. Fully synchronized in forward speeds, permits downshifting into low without a complete stop.

4-Speed fully synchronized. Extra-cost transmission has four fully synchronized forward gears: 2.52:1 first, 1.88:1 second, 1.47:1 third, 1.00:1 fourth. 2.59:1 reverse. Floor-mounted shift lever, detent reverse lockout.

Turbo Hydra-Matic. Extra-cost fully automatic three-speed transmission. Ratios: 5.06:1 to 1:1 range—drive; 5.06:1 to 1.48:1 range—low 2; 5.06:1 to 2.48:1 range—low 1; 4.24:1 to 2.08:1 range—reverse. Selector sequence: P-R-N-D-L₂-L₁.

Appearance features

Exterior. Special hood with sculptured V-shaped windsplit. Distinctive hood ornamentation. "SS 427" emblems on grille and rear deck. Special V-flagged front fender emblems. Dramatic new roof line (sport coupe). Weather-resistant vinyl-coated fabric power-operated top with glass rear window (convertible). Bright moldings around roof and lower window areas (sport coupe). Bright wheel opening and body sill moldings. Super Sport wheel covers. Triple-unit taillights with back-up lights in center.

Interior. Luxurious all-vinyl upholstery. Strato-bucket front seats with center console or Strato-back conventional seat with center armrest. Scuff-resistant plastic cowl side panels with molded-in ventilator grilles, bright metal accents on sidewalls. Bright interior garnish moldings in sport coupe. Color-keyed deep-twist carpeting. Extra-thick bright-metal-trimmed armrests with built-in finger-tip door releases. Deluxe window regulator handles. Brushed-aluminum instrument panel lower area. Electric clock. Built-in horn tabs in horizontal spokes on oval steering wheel. Cigarette lighter; built-in ashtrays in front and rear. Roof side rail lights in sport coupe. Courtesy lights in convertible and sport coupe. Automatic front door switches for dome or courtesy lights; also manual control on instrument panel. Lighted, locking glove compartment with series identification on door. Automatic luggage compartment light; patterned rubber luggage compartment mat.

Tires. Special red-stripe tires on wide-base 6" rims standard. For specific information regarding other tire sizes or appearance features, consult your Chevrolet dealer.

Extra-cost items. Comfortron air conditioning. Stereo tape system. AM/FM radio with FM stereo. Front disc brakes (includes 15" wheels and tires). Power steering, brakes and seat. Special instrumentation (tachometer, oil pressure gauge, ammeter, fuel level gauge, engine temperature gauge). Appearance Guard Group, Auxiliary Lighting Group, Operating Convenience Group, front and rear bumper guards, outside remote control rear-view mirror, shoulder belts, Strato-ease headrests for front Strato-bucket seats, rear window defroster, speed warning indicator, sports-styled steering wheel, sintered-metallic linings for drum brakes, special front and rear suspension and heavy-duty radiator. Special accent stripes. Plus many more—see your Chevrolet dealer for full details.

Interior dimensions

	Sport Coupe		Convertible	
	Front	Rear	Front	Rear
Head room	38.2"	37.4"	38.8"	37.8"
Leg room	41.7"	36.4"	42.0"	36.4"
Shoulder room	62.4"	61.0"	62.4"	53.1"
Usable luggage space (cubic feet)	17.3		17.3	

SS 427 engine (RPO L36) specifications

Engine Type	V8 Valve-in-head
Displacement (cu.-in.)	427
Bore and Stroke	4.25" x 3.76"
HP @ RPM	385 @ 5200
Torque @ RPM (ft.-lbs.)	460 @ 3400
Compression Ratio	10.25:1
Carburetion	Four-barrel/automatic choke
Camshaft	High performance
Valve Lifters	Hydraulic
Exhaust System	2½"—dual with resonators

ENGINE	TRANSMISSIONS	OPTION NO. (RPO)	REAR AXLE* STANDARD	REAR AXLE* OPTIONAL	CHASSIS SPECIFICATIONS			
385-hp Turbo-Jet 427 V8	Special 3-Speed	M13	3.31:1	3.07:1 3.55:1	Wheelbase:	119"	Tread: Front:	62.5"
	4-Speed	M20	3.31:1	3.73:1	Length:	213.2"	Rear:	62.4"
	Turbo Hydra-Matic	M40	2.73:1	3.07:1 3.31:1	Width:	79.9"		
					Height:	54.4"***		

*Positraction available for all ratios.   **Convertible—56.3"

SHOWN ON COVER (top to bottom): Corvette 427 Sport Coupe in Silver Pearl; Nova SS Sport Coupe in Ermine White; Chevelle SS 396 Sport Coupe in Granada Gold; Chevrolet SS 427 Sport Coupe in Marina Blue; and Camaro SS 350 Sport Coupe with Rally Sport option in Bolero Red with black vinyl roof cover.

IMPALA

wins Popular Science Magazine's award for the best braking of any car in the Performance Trials regardless of size, price or class!

CAMARO

out-accelerates all other cars in its class — taking first and second places.

Plus . . . Corvair proves the overall economy champ registering the best miles-per-gallon record of any car in the overall competition for the second straight year. And a Chevelle SS 396 scores first and second for gas economy in the Class VIII competition for Sport Intermediates!

CHEVROLET

SS 427
For the man who'd
buy a sports car
if it had this much room

For one thing, you want a sporting kind of engine. In this case, it's a 385-horsepower 427-cubic-inch Turbo-Jet V8, and it's standard SS 427 equipment. Sometimes, when you're not busy, you just like to sit and listen to it idle.

You like a hood that bulges. After all, you've got quite an engine under there, and you don't mind a bit if people know it. In fact, you like things that are distinctive and you know that by its very markings, the SS 427 stands apart from ordinary automobiles.

You want your car to express you just so. And happily, there's a long list of personalized touches you can add to the SS 427 — items like a new 8-track stereo tape system, front disc brakes, 4 speeds forward. Models include a Sport Coupe or Convertible.

Everything new that could happen...*happened* in styling, safety, performance

CHEVROLET

You like to unwind. So you really dig the SS 427's stiffer springs, shocks and front stabilizer bar; you know they make for better cornering. The red stripe tires mounted on the extra-wide rims help, too. All of this is standard, of course.

You're a safety-minded individual. You like the idea of the new GM-developed energy-absorbing steering column on Chevrolets. You appreciate the front seat belt retractors and the folding front seat back latches — all standard.

You especially appreciate a dual master cylinder brake system — with a warning light to advise you of a pressure imbalance in either part of the system. You're glad that all other '67 Chevrolets carry the system, too, along with corrosion-resistant brake lines.

New Chevrolet SS 427 Sport Coupe (Convertible, too) now performing at your Chevrolet dealer's.

'67 CHEVROLET

MARK OF EXCELLENCE

Engineering Details

Here are the facts and figures that make the 1967 Chevrolets the most rewarding we've ever built. Study them over or just give them a glance. Either way you'll know these new Chevrolets are cars you can depend on.

CHEVROLET POWER TEAM CHART FOR '67

STANDARD ENGINES	Standard Transmission	Extra-Cost Optional Transmissions			
	3-Speed Fully Synchronized	Overdrive	4-Speed Fully Synchronized	Powerglide	Turbo Hydra-Matic
155-hp Turbo-Thrift 250 Six†	•	•		•	
195-hp Turbo-Fire 283 V8	•	•	•	•	
EXTRA-COST OPTIONAL ENGINES					
275-hp Turbo-Fire 327 V8	•		•	•	•**
325-hp Turbo-Jet 396 V8	*		•	•	•
385-hp Turbo-Jet 427 V8	*		•		•

†Not offered for Caprice Models. *Extra-cost special 3-Speed Fully Synchronized transmission must be specified.
**Caprice and Impala models only.

SAFETY FEATURES STANDARD ON ALL '67 CHEVROLET-BUILT CARS

Front seat shoulder belt anchors * Padded instrument panel * Padded sun visors * Four-way hazard warning flasher * Dual master cylinder brake system with warning light * Dual-speed windshield wipers * Windshield washer * Back-up lights * Outside rearview mirror * Tire safety rim * Seat belts—front and rear with pushbutton buckles * Energy-absorbing steering column * Passenger-guard door locks—all doors * Folding seat back latches (wagons) * Folding front seat back latches (2-doors) * Inside day-night mirror with shatter-resistant vinyl-edged glass and breakaway support * Lane-change feature incorporated in direction signal control * Corrosion-resistant brake lines * Energy-absorbing steering wheel * Energy-absorbing instrument panel with smooth contoured knobs and levers * Soft, low-profile window control knobs, and coat hooks * Front seat belt retractors * Safety door latches and hinges * Uniform shift quadrant (PRNDL) * Thick laminate windshield * Reduced glare instrument panel and windshield wiper arms and blades.

ENGINES

Whether you cozy around town or cruise the pikes, Chevrolet builds a number of engines to meet your exact performance needs. Fact is, you can go it with a standard Six or V8—depending on the model you choose—or you can order one of several extra-cost V8s with up to 385 horses. Whatever your decision, you should know that all Chevrolet engines feature high-strength precision castings engineered to precise tolerances, efficient overhead valves, wedge-shaped combustion chambers, short inlet and exhaust ports, controlled pressure lubrication system with full-flow filter, pressurized cooling system and high-capacity water pump. Fuel induction system tailored to engine. New on both standard Six and V8 this year is a starter motor which, when coupled with Chevrolet's new energizer-type battery, kicks over the engine at higher rpm for quicker starts. A 24-gallon fuel tank and a more accurate fuel gauge sending unit for all sedans, coupes and convertibles are also new in 1967. And there's a wide selection of rear axle ratios for performance the way you like it.

STANDARD ENGINES

(Depending on model selected.)

155-HP TURBO-THRIFT 250 SIX. Modern design of this economical engine trims front-end weight for easy handling. In addition, a compression ratio of 8.5:1, single-barrel carburetor, automatic choke, short-stroke design and economy-contoured camshaft provide unusual efficiency and thrift. Seven main bearings and fully counterweighted crankshaft encourage long engine life and smooth operation.

195-HP TURBO-FIRE 283 V8. Lots of action in this popular V8, yet it won't throw your gas budget out of kilter. Chevrolet components include two-barrel carburetor with automatic choke, hydraulic valve lifters, positive-type engine ventilation, oil-wetted polyurethane air filter and general-performance camshaft. 9.25:1 compression ratio.

EXTRA-COST ENGINES

275-HP TURBO-FIRE 327 V8. 275 horses chocked into 327 cu. in. here. Features include a high compression ratio of 10.0:1, four-barrel carburetor with automatic choke, hydraulic valve lifters, general-performance camshaft and large single exhaust system. Comes with a huskier transmission support. Available on all full-size Chevrolets.

325-HP TURBO-JET 396 V8. This big-bore V8 may also be specified for all '67 Chevrolets. Has a four-barrel carburetor with automatic choke, hydraulic valve lifters and large single exhaust system. Valves, valve ports and combustion chambers are engineered for optimum volumetric efficiency. Compression ratio is 10.25:1.

385-HP TURBO-JET 427 V8. This plant utilizes the same basic design configuration as the Turbo-Jet 396. Starting with a whopping 427 cubic inches, it comes by 385 horses this way: performance-rated four-barrel carburetor, automatic choke, high-performance camshaft, hydraulic lifters, 10.25:1 compression ratio and dual exhaust system with resonators. Can be ordered on all full-size Chevrolets.

TRANSMISSIONS

Chevrolet offers you a wide range of both manual and automatic gearboxes this year—from sporty manual varieties to silent self-shifters. For information on availability of specific transmissions with engines, see the power team chart on this page.

3-SPEED FULLY SYNCHRONIZED. Standard on all full-size '67 Chevrolets, though a special heavy-duty version must be ordered for Turbo-Jet V8s. On top of being quick and quiet, you can shift down into first without coming to a stop—all forward gears are synchronized. Plenty tough, too, because it totes wide helical gears, large synchronizers and high-capacity front and rear ball bearings. New shift lever on the steering column.

4-SPEED FULLY SYNCHRONIZED. There's no wasted motion with this floor-mounted quickshifter. All helical gear design, fully synchronized in all forward gears. Slips into all gears smoothly. This sporty arrangement can be ordered with any Chevrolet V8.

AUTOMATIC POWERGLIDE. Three-element torque converter and hydraulically coordinated two-speed planetary gearset provide exceptionally clean shifts. In low-speed passing situations, press down on the accelerator and automatically shift into low. Five-position selector reads Park-R-N-D-L: Parking-Reverse-Neutral-Drive-Low. Straight-line selection is featured on models having floor-mounted shift lever (standard with front bucket seats). This transmission may be ordered with six-cylinder models and all V8s except the 385-hp Turbo-Jet.

AUTOMATIC TURBO HYDRA-MATIC. Nearly instantaneous response and quiet operation brand this versatile automatic. Employs a three-element torque converter plus a compound three-speed planetary gearset arrangement to shift through three forward speed ranges. Can be downshifted for engine braking or accelerated passing at speeds below 70 mph. Six-position selector dial reads Park-R-N-D-L2-L1: Parking-Reverse-Neutral-Drive-Low 2 (for bumper-to-bumper, stop-and-go traffic)-Low 1 (for steep grades). Turbo Hydra-Matic can be specified with the 275-hp, 325-hp and 385-hp Turbo-Jet V8s. (See chart above.) Features floor-mounted shift lever in bucket seat models.

OVERDRIVE. Available with either standard V8 or Six. A fully synchronized 3-Speed with 2-speed planetary unit lowers engine speed to reduce engine wear and drop fuel consumption. Comes into play semi-automatically at about 30 mph. A T-handle activation control is located under the instrument panel.

CLUTCH. Chevrolet's single disc dry clutch with positive action diaphragm springs is matched to specific engine performance for easy shifting and durability. Includes lifetime lubricated release bearing and light aluminum alloy housing. Standard Six and V8 have units with spring-loaded diaphragms. Clutches on standard V8 with 4-Speed transmission and on extra-cost V8s are centrifugally assisted.

SPECIFICATIONS

Wheelbase ....119.0"
Width, overall ....79.9"
Length, overall
    Station wagons ....212.4"
    Other models ....213.2"
Tread
    Station wagons...front 63.5".....rear 63.4"
    Other models ....front 62.5".....rear 62.4"
Height, loaded
    Sedans .... 55.4"
    Sport sedans .... 54.5"
    Sport coupes .... 54.4"
    Convertibles .... 55.3"
    Station wagons .... 56.7"

1968

Chevrolet and the rest of the industry rebounded this year from the sales showing of the previous year. Still far below its 1965 sales high, Chevy calendar year sales were up a gratifying 5% to 2,148,091.

The Impala SS was clearly nearing the end of the trail. It was now classified for the first time since 1963 as a subseries of the Impala. It was available on the Sport Coupe, Custom Coupe and Converetible as RPO Z03. Hidaway windshield wipers made their Impala debute this year along with side marker lamps. All Impalas had triple taillights mounted in the bumper. An SS was identified by the black-accented grille with SS nameplates on the grille, front fenders and rear deck lid. No SS identification was carried on the wheelcovers which were standard Impala issue although some nice optional ones were available. Strato-bucket seats with center console and head restraints came with the SS package. There was SS identification on the steering wheel hub.

The SS 427 was carried over this year despite the disappointing sales of the year before. The SS 427 package was again built around the top-of-the-performance-line 385-hp 427 V-8 engine. The package included special exterior identification which included three vertical front fender louvers, the domed hood with vertical air scoop below and parallel to the windshield and the front marker lamp bezels with "427" ID.

The Caprice continued to offer the Coupe and Sedan models plus station wagon. The Caprice Coupe carried the dubious distinction of being the first of the big Chevrolets to eliminate side vent windows (one was apparently to be consoled by the fact that according to GM your comfort had not been sacrificed in vain, those nasty old vent windows could no longer "inter-

rupt Caprice Coupe's classic lines.") Added this year were concealed headlights.

The Bel Air and Biscayne continued to be offered only in Sedan and station wagon models.

Length was 214.7" and height was 79.6". The top rated engine was the 427 with 385-hp. A new 327 V-8 was offered, the 250-hp Turbo-Fire with 8.75:1 compression. The new standard V-8 was a 307 rated at 200-hp with 9:1 compression and 2-bbl carburetion. An Impala SS could still be ordered with the standard 250 Turbo-Thrift 155-hp Six although Caprice, Impala Convertibles and Custom Coupes were only available with a V-8.

Model year production totalled an estimated 1,236,300 of which 82,100 were Biscaynes (37,600 with V-8); 152,200 were Bel Airs (123,400 with V-8); 710,900 were Impalas (699,500 with V-8 and 38,210 with the SS option and 1,778 with SS427 optional equipment); 115,500 were Caprice; and 175,600 were wagons (167,900 with V-8).

The least expensive Chevrolet this year (excluding station wagons) was the Biscayne two-door sedan with a base price of $2,686 (3,514 lbs.) and the most expensive was the Caprice hardtop sedan with a base price of $3,271 (3,754 lbs.). The Bel Air two-door sedan was base priced at $2,786 (3,518 lbs.) and the Impala four-door sedan carried a base tag of $2,951 (3,623 lbs.). The Impala hardtop sedan was base priced at $3,022 (3,711 lbs.).

Literature this year consisted of full-line brochure and the big Chevys brochure (pages 118-121 and 126). A mailer catalogue, "Q & A", was issued (pages 124-125) and there was a football-related catalogue featuring high performance Chevys (pages 122-123). Somewhat surprising in light of the imminent decline of the SS, it was well covered in the literature.

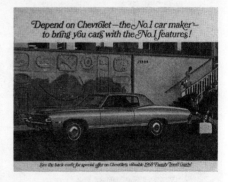

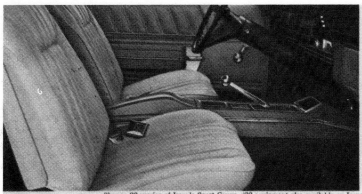 

Shown: SS version of Impala Sport Coupe. (SS equipment also available on Impala Custom Coupe.)

Impala SS Coupe

Specify the SS version of an Impala Coupe and you've got a car that's
Something Special. Outside, take your pick of roof lines—classic Custom Coupe
or sweptback Sport Coupe. Inside, it's driver's choice. A color selection of
all-vinyl interiors are available for bucket-seat fans. Handsome center console
with storage compartment divides the buckets. Special upholstery is of
tufted vertical vinyl pleats with contrasting trim. Stand out even more from
the crowd by blending in the SS 427 package that you can order. It includes
simulated hood intake, SS 427 emblems, red stripe (or white stripe) wide-oval
tires, 15″ x 6″ wheels, special suspension components, large-diameter front
stabilizer bar and, finally, what it's really all about, the 385-hp Turbo-Jet
427 V8 engine.

Impala SS Convertible

For the ultimate in topdown travel, specify the Impala SS Convertible. Put yourself completely in command by ordering the fully synchronized 4-Speed gearbox. Or elect the Turbo Hydra-Matic and get a two-way unit: it shifts for itself through three forward ranges, or lets you shift for yourself. Go with the new standard 200-hp V8 or specify one of four other V8s with up to 385 horsepower (that 385-hp V8 gives you the basis to order the SS 427 package, too). Bring it to a halt with smooth fade-resistant stopping power by ordering refined front wheel disc brakes. Inside, Strato-bucket seats, center console and all the other SS package goodies. As with all '68 Chevrolets, you're getting that solid sound- and weather-insulated Body by Fisher, Full Coil suspension and cushion-mounted power team.

Shown above: Impala SS Convertible with SS 427 equipment you can order.

Slim-waisted new looks. Half again as quiet inside.
An even more road-sure ride.

There's fresh new styling with a formal roof line, recessed triple
taillights, Hide-A-Way wipers. New quietness, because we
put rubber cushions and thick insulation everywhere noise and

'68 Impala SS
from Chevrolet's Sports Department

1968 Impala SS Custom Coupe

vibration might get through. An ever surer ride: wide-stanced, full-coiled and poised. SS—the Impala with bucket seats, center console and young notions.

1968 CHEVROLET POWER TEAMS

	Standard Transmission	Extra-Cost Transmissions				
	3-Speed fully synch.	Special 3-Speed fully synch.	Overdrive	4-Speed fully synch.	Powerglide	Turbo Hydra-Matic
Standard Engines						
155-hp Turbo-Thrift 250 Six†	●		●	●	●	
200-hp Turbo-Fire 307 V8	●		●	●	●	O
Extra-Cost Engines						
250-hp Turbo-Fire 327 V8	●			●	●	●
275-hp Turbo-Fire 327 V8	●			●	●	●
325-hp Turbo-Jet 396 V8		●		●	●	●
385-hp Turbo-Jet 427 V8		●		●		●

Center console with versatile 4-speed shift

What a '68 Chevrolet Means to You on the Technical Side

ENGINES

Chevrolet's engine lineup for 1968 has been expanded to offer you a greater variety of power choices. Move out smartly with Chevrolet's standard Six or V8 (depending on the model you pick) or order one of four other V8s up to 385 horsepower. Every Chevrolet engine gives you these significant features: high-strength precision castings engineered to precise tolerances, efficient overhead valves with hydraulic lifters, wedge-shaped combustion chambers, short inlet and exhaust ports, controlled pressure lubrication system with full-flow filter, pressurized cooling system and high-capacity water pump. Fuel induction systems are tailored to suit the engine. All '68 engines are equipped with exhaust emission control equipment. All engines are fed by a large 24-gallon fuel tank for longer distances between gas stops.

STANDARD ENGINES (Depending on model selected)

155-HP TURBO-THRIFT 250 SIX. This advanced-design engine has single-barrel carburetor, automatic choke, short-stroke design and economy-contoured camshaft—all combine to make this a most frugal and efficient engine. Improved water pump sealing, fully counterweighted crankshaft and seven main bearings are but a few of the features that insure smooth, long-lasting performance and dependable Chevrolet operation.

200-HP TURBO-FIRE 307 V8. New for 1968, this rugged, more powerful engine replaces the previous 195-hp 283-cu.-in. engine as the standard V8 for all Chevrolets. It retains all the reliability and economy of its predecessor through two-barrel carburetor with automatic choke, positive-type engine ventilation, general performance camshaft. The 9.0:1 compression ratio means you can use a regular-grade fuel for savings.

EXTRA-COST ENGINES

250-HP TURBO-FIRE 327 V8. Also new for '68, this version of the popular 327 V8 engine stresses economy of operation. It has an 8.75:1 compression ratio to burn regular-grade fuel, four-barrel carburetor with automatic choke, and general performance camshaft.

275-HP TURBO-FIRE 327 V8. A favorite of Chevrolet fans, this engine is packed with durability and performance. It has four-barrel carburetor with automatic choke, general performance camshaft, large diameter single exhaust system and 10.0:1 compression ratio.

325-HP TURBO-JET 396 V8. Turbo-Jet design puts exceptional responsiveness under the hood. Four-barrel carburetor, automatic choke and large diameter single exhaust system are only a few of its attributes. Unique to the Turbo-Jet engines are the extra-strong crankshaft supports affording longer engine life, and advanced-engineered valve system and combustion chambers for maximum efficiency at all engine speeds. Compression ratio: 10.25:1.

385-HP TURBO-JET 427 V8. Chevrolet's top power for '68. Complementing its 427-cu.-in. displacement: performance-rated four-barrel carburetor, automatic choke, high-performance camshaft, 10.25:1 compression ratio, dual exhaust system with resonators.

TRANSMISSIONS

Chevrolet has a transmission for every driver—whether he is a shift-it-yourselfer or one that likes the car to do it for him. There's even a transmission that will please both types.

3-SPEED FULLY SYNCHRONIZED. Standard on all '68 Chevrolets (depending on engine). Fully synchronized means you can manually downshift into first at low speeds without coming to a full stop. Wide helical gears, large synchronizers and high-capacity front and rear bearings make this transmission rugged and quiet.

OVERDRIVE. Available with standard Six or V8. This fully synchronized 3-speed unit has a 2-speed planetary gear feature which reduces engine speed, causing a decrease in wear and an increase in gas mileage. Shifts into Overdrive automatically at about 30 mph. A control on the instrument panel enables you to lock out Overdrive when desired.

SPECIAL 3-SPEED FULLY SYNCHRONIZED. This special-duty version of the standard 3-speed transmission is designed for higher performance engines and must be specified with the Turbo-Jet V8s when a manual 3-speed unit is wanted.

4-SPEED FULLY SYNCHRONIZED. For sportiness and versatility, order four-on-the-floor with any Chevrolet V8. You get smooth responsive shifts through all-helical gears. Each forward gear is fully synchronized. The new shift control lever has a simple spring device to prevent shifting into reverse accidentally, replacing the manually released spring lockout.

AUTOMATIC POWERGLIDE. Long a Chevrolet favorite, this transmission has a 3-element torque converter and hydraulically controlled 2-speed planetary gearset. It adds up to smooth acceleration and quiet, dependable performance at a modest price. An accelerator-actuated automatic mechanism enables downshifts into low range. The five-position selector reads Park-R-N-D-L. When the center console-mounted shift lever is ordered, a new inverted-U-shaped lever selects the gears. A detent bar on the lever's underside prevents accidental movement of the selector into R, L or Park.

AUTOMATIC TURBO HYDRA-MATIC. The most you could want in an automatic transmission. Shifts for itself quickly and silk smooth. Or make it happen by moving the selector lever through the three forward gear ranges. It all occurs because of a 3-element torque converter with a compound 3-speed planetary gearset arrangement. This means sure automatic shifts. It also downshifts—automatically—for passing power or engine braking. Merely press down on the accelerator when you're in mid-speedometer speed range. With the center console, selector lever is of the new inverted-U-shape design. A new 2.56:1 economy rear axle ratio is available with this transmission.

24

Sales turned down for the industry this year and Chevrolet was not exempt. Calendar year sales fell to 1,999,256.

New bodies appeared this year throughout the line. The new sheet metal created a bulkier appearance. With GM pursuing its perfidious policy to a Final Solution, side window vents were gone for good from the entire line.

The SS 427 option was retained for one last year. It was available as an option on the Custom Coupe, Sport Coupe or Convertible for $422. An Impala e-quipped with the SS 427 option was identified from the outside by the SS emblems carried on the black-accented grille, front fenders and rear deck. Tires were red-striped G70's on 15" wheels.

Interior appointments for the SS were not substan-tially different from that of a standard Impala model. Bucket seats came with a console which housed the stick or selector lever but the seats and console were options, not standard equipment. Basically all the interior you got was an SS identification on the steering wheel.

The Caprice continued to be Chevrolet's luxury model and came loaded with significantly upgraded interior upholstery. Caprice and Impala shared the triple taillight arrangement. The Caprice was only available with a V-8 engine.

The Bel Air and Biscayne were offered only in two- and four-door sedan models. They shared twin tail-light arrangements.

This year Chevrolet reversed itself and went back to naming its station wagons the way it had prior to 1962: Biscayne wagons were named Brookwoods; Bel Air wagons were Townsmans (Townsmen?); Impala wagons were Kingswoods; and Caprice wagons were Kingswood Estates (they had simulated wood-trim, wouldn't you know).

The new sheet metal rested on the 119" wheelbase, however overall length was up to 215.9" (216.7" on the station wagons) and height increased to 79.8". Engine availability was again topped by the 390-hp 427 V-8 Turbo-Jet. The extra 5-hp over 1968 was achieved by modifying the cylinder heads and pis-tons. The base six was the 250 Turbo-Thrift turning 155-hp. Also available were the standard V-8, 235-hp 327 and optional 255-hp 350, 300-hp 350, 265-hp 396

and 335-hp 427. The three-speed M13 transmission was standard with the SS 427 and two four-speed trans-missions (2.52:1 and 2.20:1) plus Turbo Hydra-Matic were optional. A three-speed (non heavy-duty) was standard on all other models, a four-speed was op-tional and Powerglide was available on all but Im-pala SS 427 models. The transmission innovation this year was the variable-ratio power assist power steering (19.3:1/15.5:1) on Caprice and Impala mo-dels.

Model year production was 1,190,000. Of these 68,700 were Biscayne (41,300 with V-8); 155,700 were Bel Air (139,700 with V-8); 777,000 were Impala (768,300 with V-8 and only 2,455 or 2,425 (estimates vary) were equipped with the SS 427 option); and 166,900 were Caprice. Separate station wagon produc-tion totals are not available.

The least expensive Chevrolet this year (excluding station wagons) was the two-door Biscayne sedan base priced at $2,751 (3,670 lbs.) and the most expensive was the Caprice hardtop sport sedan base priced at $3,346 (3,895 lbs.). The Bel Air two-door sedan was base priced at $2,851 (3,675 lbs.) while an Impala four-door sedan carried a base tag of $3,016 (3,760 lbs.). The Impala hardtop sport sedan cost $3,086 (3,855 lbs.).

Literature was plentiful this year. There was, of course, the full-line Chevrolet catalogue (cover shown below) as well as the big Chevys catalogue (pages 128-129 and 138). In addition, there were several sport related pieces issued. One piece was a Hula Bowl promotion (cover below) and another was a small piece honoring "College Football's 100th Sea-son" (pages 130-131). The Chevrolet "Sports Dept." issued a catalogue entitled, "Where you get the Chevrolet Viewpoint on all our Sports Models," that fully illustrated the SS 427 option (pages 132-135). The Chevrolet "Sports-Recreation Dept." also issued a catalogue, probably a mailer, that did not illus-trate any high performance big Chevys. A full-line catalogue called "The Chevrolet Viewpoint 1969" was issued which did not mention or illustrate them, either (cover below). A "Value Showdown" mailer catalogue, however, did have a spread that mentioned the 427 (pages 136-137).

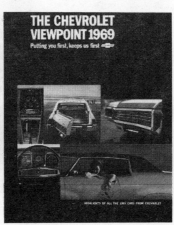

It's the silent ones who are usually strongest when the convertible is a good example. Its Body by Fisher is tough to

going gets rough. This SS 427
shake and even harder to rattle.

Some of the equipment illustrated is optional at extra cost 9

'69 Impala SS 427

About all that's left for its rivals to offer you is

Up to now sport like this was something you splurged on. But look at what this robust new Impala brings you at a Chevrolet price. Clean-honed styling subtleties like the extended loop-around bumper line on the custom coupe above. Comforts like Astro Ventilation in every model. Engineering niceties like variable-ratio power steering you can order for quicker, virtually

Chevrolet introduces 1969.
The year of the Super Sports.
Galaxy Football's 10th Season.
The Chevrolet Sports Department

excuses.

effortless maneuvering. Even headlights that wash themselves—a new push-button assist available for better visibility. And it's all set in motion by a 427-cu.-in. Turbo-Jet V8 that turns out up to 390-hp. SS 427. Three-quarters pure luxury. Three-quarters pure sport. If you figure that adds up to a car and a half —you're right.

CHEVROLET

Putting you first keeps us first

SS 427

THE CHEVROLET SPORTS DEPARTMENT

SS 427

Enter the hybrid SS 427. It crosses a luxury car with flat cornering and strong performance. Strictly big-sport class in custom coupe, sport coupe and convertible.

APPEARANCE FEATURES

EXTERIOR—First, you select your SS 427 in the basic Impala body style you want: the custom coupe, the sport coupe or the convertible. Each model carries such Impala marks as full door-glass styling, Hide-A-Way windshield wipers and vinyl-insert side moldings. Then, here's what you get outside as SS 427 extras. Black-accented grille and SS identification on grille, front fenders and deck lid. Wide-oval red-stripes on 15-inch wheels. Under the hood—427-cubic-inches.

INTERIOR—SS identification on steering wheel. Order bucket seats and you get a center console and shift lever on the console with automatic or 4-Speed. Two head restraints with all front seats. Astro Ventilation with large rectangular vent-ports in face of instrument panel. Interior air exhausts through door pillar vents. Ignition switch now located on steering column. Remove the key and a sliding-type bolt locks steering shaft. Shift lever and ignition are locked, too.

MECHANICAL FEATURES

ENGINES—SS (RPO Z24) comes with a 390-hp 427-cu.-in. V8 under the hood. This 427 engine is of the "porcupine head" design. This arrangement locates the valves directly in line with the gas flow. Intake and exhaust passages are individually ported. Thick main bearing bulkheads and wide bearing caps contribute to the durability and superb performance reputation of these engines. A few of the refinements this year include a more efficient and durable cooling fan; improved fueling and filtering. "Inboard balancing" locates accessories closer to engine block for smoother, durable operation.

TRANSMISSIONS—*Special 3-Speed* fully synchro-nized heavy-duty transmission standard with SS 427; column-mounted lever. *4-Speed* fully synchronized transmission available with either wide- or close-ratio gear spacing. Floor-mounted lever. All manual transmissions have a starter safety switch. *Turbo Hydra-Matic* fully automatic 3-speed with torque converter. Quadrant markings for sport-type manual shifting to let engine wind tighter in gears if desired. Selector lever mounted in console when so equipped; on column without console.

CHASSIS-SUSPENSION-REAR AXLE—Perimeter-type frame with torque-box design and four crossmembers. Fully independent front suspension with stiffer springs and stabilizer bar. Single-piston-caliper, power-assisted front disc brakes come with SS 427. Better handling with new steering linkage. New variable-ratio power steering available; gives faster turning response in tight parking and maneuvering; retains excellent road feel on the highway. Link-type rear suspension with two upper and two lower control arms; coil springs. Computer-selected springs for proper car height and trim. Quieter, more durable universal joints.

POPULAR EXTRA-COST OPTIONS ☐ Headlight washers with nozzles pointed at each outboard lens to rinse away grime ☐ Stereo tape system ☐ AM/FM and AM/FM stereo radios ☐ Air conditioning systems with improved cooling efficiency ☐ Soft-Ray tinted glass ☐ Electrically heated rear window for defrosting on custom coupe ☐ Comfortilt steering wheel ☐ Map light integral with rearview mirror ☐ Wheel covers ☐ Wheel trim rings ☐ Rally wheels ☐ Power steering, windows and seats ☐ Heavy-duty electrical and suspension equipment ☐ Positraction ☐ Trailer-towing equipment ☐ Vinyl roof cover ☐ Engine block heater.

SS 427 POWER TEAMS

ENGINE	TRANSMISSION	REAR AXLE RATIO (:1)*			
		Std.	Optional		
			Econ.	Perf.	Spcl.
Turbo-Jet 427 427-Cu.-In. V8 390 HP @ 5400 4-bbl. carb. 10.25:1 C.R. Premium Fuel	Special 3-Speed (2.42:1 Low)	3.31	3.07	3.55	3.73
	4-Speed (2.52:1 Low)				
	4-Speed (2.20:1 Low)				
	Turbo Hydra-Matic	2.73		3.07	2.29

*Without Air Conditioning. Positraction required for 3.73; optional all others.

SS 427 GRILLE

RALLY WHEEL

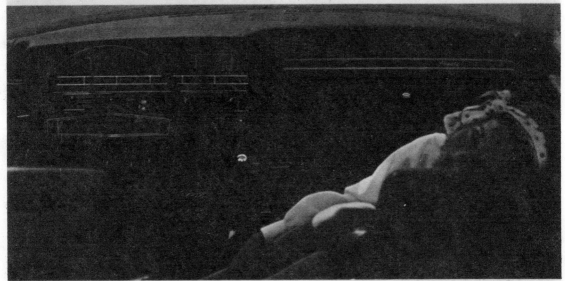

SS 427 INSTRUMENT PANEL AND STEERING WHEEL

SS 427 INTERIOR WITH BUCKET SEATS AND CONSOLE

Match this!

The biggest
base six
and V8 engines
in the field.

Chevrolet
Cubic inch displacement is an important measure of engine capacity. And judged by this measure, Chevrolet clearly out-classes its rivals in both the six and V8 categories. And remember, we're talking about the thrifty, regular gas base engines, not extra-cost equipment. But when you get to available engines, Chevrolet offers the most powerful in its field, the 427 Turbo-Jet 390-hp V8.

Other significant items include a side guard beam built into every door. It looks like one of those guard rails you see along the freeway, and not only strengthens the door but puts a more solid wall between you and the outside world. Still another feature, a steel cargo

1969

Show up for the Chevrolet
Value Showdown at your
Chevrolet dealer's . . . now

guard between trunk and passenger compartments to help protect passengers and trunk contents.

Of course we'll stack up the looks of Chevrolet with anything around at any price. And why not gather together the family and stage a sit-in in a Chevrolet interior?

There's something even better about Chevrolet's famous Full Coil ride. We go to the trouble of programming each car's equipment load into an electronic computer. The computer then tells us exactly which springs to use, depending on the car's weight and which way it's distributed. What's more, this is the longest Chevrolet ever built, with plenty of sound-deadening insulation. Pretty smooth? Drive it and see.

CHEVROLET IMPALA SPORT SEDAN

Chevrolet performance: It moves you deeply

If Chevrolet's choice of engines and transmissions seems bewilderingly large, it's because we've tried to anticipate just about every driving requirement. Result: a perfect match of engine and transmission choices.

STANDARD ENGINES (depending upon model selected)

155-hp Turbo-Thrift 250 Six. Nurses a gallon of gasoline along as if it were never going to see another one. Single-barrel carburetor, automatic choke, short-stroke design and economy contoured camshaft. Also improved water pump sealing, fully counterweighted crankshaft and seven main crankshaft bearings. You don't have to write all this down; just ask for the Six.

235-hp Turbo-Fire 327 V8. A heftier Standard V8 for '69. Performs beautifully on regular fuel. Compression ratio: 9.00:1, two-barrel carburetor, automatic choke and general performance camshaft.

EXTRA-COST ENGINES

255-hp Turbo-Fire 350 V8. One of two 350-cube V8 engines. And it does a fantastic job on regular fuel. Compression ratio: 9.00:1, four-barrel carburetor, automatic choke and general performance camshaft.

300-hp Turbo-Fire 350 V8. The premium gas and premium performance 350 version. Compression ratio: 10.25:1, four-barrel carburetor, automatic choke and high performance camshaft.

265-hp Turbo-Jet 396 V8. Regular fuel economy with big-inch V8 performance. Compression ratio: 9.00:1, two-barrel carburetor, automatic choke and high performance camshaft.

335-hp Turbo-Jet 427 V8. Great from the word "Go!" Compression ratio: 10.25:1, four-barrel carburetor, automatic choke and high performance camshaft.

390-hp Turbo-Jet 427 V8. The King. Compression 10.25:1, four-barrel carburetor, automatic choke and high performance camshaft.

TRANSMISSIONS

3-speed Fully Synchronized. Standard on all Chevrolets (with standard engines). Synchronizing allows downshift into first gear without coming to a full stop. Wide helical gears, high-capacity front and rear bearings. On models equipped with manual transmission the engine will not start until the clutch is disengaged.

Special 3-speed Fully Synchronized. Specifically designed for higher output V8s. Required (when 3-speed manual transmission is preferred) with 350, 396 and 427 V8s.

4-speed Fully Synchronized. Mostly for the fun of it. Available with all V8s. New for all manual transmissions: clutch must be depressed before the engine will start.

Powerglide. The smoothest two-speed automatic shifting available anywhere. Three-element torque converter and two-speed planetary gearset. May be ordered with all engines but 396 and 427 V8s.

Turbo Hydra-matic. Gives you a choice of effortless automatic shifting or you can shift it yourself through the three forward gear ratios. Torque converter with three-speed planetary gearset. "Stirrup-type" selector lever when ordered with centre console. Available with all engines.

Clutch. Carefully matched to engine output. Single dry disc design with release bearing sealed in lubricant and a light aluminum alloy housing. Also available: new double-disc heavy-duty clutch.

Exhaust Emission Control. Exhaust gases are reburned to reduce air pollutants. Air injection reactor used with manual transmissions; controlled combustion system with automatic transmissions.

1969 CHEVROLET POWER TEAMS					
	3-speed fully synchronized	Special 3-speed fully synchronized	4-speed fully synchronized	Powerglide	Turbo Hydra-matic
155-hp Turbo-Thrift 250*	●			●	●
235-hp Turbo-Fire 327 V8*	●		●	●	●
255-hp Turbo-Fire 350 V8		●	●	●	●
300-hp Turbo-Fire 350 V8		●	●	●	●
265-hp Turbo-Jet 396 V8		●	●		●
335-hp Turbo-Jet 427 V8		●	●		●
390-hp Turbo-Jet 427 V8		●	●		●

*Standard Engine. Turbo-Thrift 250 (six) not available on Caprice models, Impala Custom Coupe or Convertible.

1970

The new model year of 1970 brought with it more than just the beginning and end of a decade. It marked the beginning and the end of an era. While it would take another year or so for the impending, inevitable economic, regulatory and insurance forces to prevail, the musclecar era was over for Chevy.

The Impala SS and the SS 427 were gone. The

Biscayne, Bel Air, Impala and Caprice offerings were standard family fare. Base engines were the 350 V-8 and the 250 Six.

We have reproduced an excerpt from the main catalogue on pages 140-143 to close out the story of a once-great performance tradition.

Chevrolet Impala Custom Coupe

You get a bigger standard V8 engine – 350 cu.-in.

The new standard V8 is a lot of engine.
So is the standard Six.

But there may be times you'll want performance over and above what either of those has to offer.

V8s up to 454 cubic inches, for instance. (And two of those.)

Others with two-barrel carburetion that run beautifully on regular-grade fuel.

All engines for 1970 have new transmission-controlled spark advance for smoother acceleration and improved emission control. And new slim-line gasketless spark plugs for the Six and Turbo-Jet V8s.

Here is rather complete information on the standard engines, and others you can order.

Standard engines

155-hp Turbo-Thrift 250 Six.*
What this does to a dollar's worth of gas is what should be done to a dollar's worth of gas. Makes it last.

Single-barrel carburetor, automatic choke, short-stroke design and economy-contoured camshaft. Features fully counterweighted crankshaft and seven main bearings.

New 250-hp Turbo-Fire 350 V8.
A larger, more powerful standard V8 for 1970.

Compression ratio 9.00:1. Two-barrel carburetion, automatic choke, general-performance camshaft.

And regular fuel, yet.

Extra-cost engines

300-hp Turbo-Fire 350 V8.
The four-barrel carburetor version of the standard 350-cubic-inch V8.

Premium fuel.

Compression ratio 10.25:1. Automatic choke and general-performance camshaft.

265-hp Turbo-Fire 400 V8.
New low-weight, small-block, large-displacement V8. 9.00:1 compression ratio. Two-barrel carburetor.

Regular fuel. Yes, regular fuel.

Automatic choke. General-performance camshaft.

345-hp Turbo-Jet 454 V8.
Compression ratio 10.25:1. Premium fuel. Four-barrel carburetion. Automatic choke and general-performance camshaft.

390-hp Turbo-Jet 454 V8.
Mr. Big.

Compression ratio 10.25:1. Premium fuel. Four-barrel carburetion. Automatic choke and general-performance camshaft.

Transmissions

Turbo Hydra-matic.
The choice is yours—effortless automatic shifting or you can shift for yourself through three forward ranges.

Powerglide.
The smoothest two-speed automatic shifting available anywhere.

And the long-time favorite among Chevrolet owners.

3-Speed Fully Synchronized.
Standard on all Big Chevrolets (with standard engines).

Synchronizing allows downshift into first gear without coming to a full stop. Wide helical gears, high-capacity front and rear bearings.

Safety feature: clutch must be depressed before starting engine.

Facts, Figures and Specifications

Wheelbase	119.0″
Length (overall)	216.0″
Width (overall)	79.8″
Height (loaded):	
Caprice Coupe & Impala Custom Coupe	54.2″
Caprice Sedan & Impala Sport Sedan	54.5″
Impala Sport Coupe	54.7″
Impala Convertible	54.6″
Impala & Bel Air 4-Door Sedans	55.5″
Front Tread	63.4″
Rear Tread	63.3″
Fuel tank rated capacity (Gallons)	24

Tire Size & Steering Specifications

Standard tire size	
(Depending on model)	F78 x 15, G78 x 15
Turning circle, curb-to-curb (ft.)	41.0
Turning circle, wall-to-wall (ft.)	43.0
Steering ratio, standard (overall)	30.7:1
Steering ratio, power (overall)	19.3:1—15.5:1

Power Teams			
Engines	Transmissions		
	3-Speed	Powerglide	Turbo Hydra-matic
155-hp Turbo-Thrift 250 Six*	•	•	•
250-hp Turbo-Fire 350 V8*	•	•	•
300-hp Turbo-Fire 350 V8		•	•
265-hp Turbo-Fire 400 V8		•	•
345-hp Turbo-Jet 454 V8			•
390-hp Turbo-Jet 454 V8			•

*Standard. Six not available with Caprice models, Impala Custom Coupe, Sport Sedan or Convertible.

22

You always get what's coming to you when you trade your Chevrolet. More.

Chevrolet Impala Convertible

Go your own way.

We mentioned on page 4 there are eight ways to go.

That's not entirely accurate.

By selecting the additional equipment you want, chances are very good you'll have a Big Chevrolet unlike anyone else's.

Here is a brief checklist you can use to help make up your own Chevrolet.

Your Chevrolet dealer has a complete list of Options and Custom Features plus information on availability.

Model_____

Interiors

- ☐ Caprice custom knit nylon and vinyl
- ☐ Caprice brocade cloth and vinyl
- ☐ Pattern cloth and vinyl
- ☐ All-vinyl (standard on convertible, available for some other models)

Engines

- ☐ 155-hp Turbo-Thrift 250 Six*
- ☐ 250-hp Turbo-Fire 350 V8*
- ☐ 300-hp Turbo-Fire 350 V8
- ☐ 265-hp Turbo-Fire 400 V8
- ☐ 345-hp Turbo-Jet 454 V8
- ☐ 390-hp Turbo-Jet 454 V8

Standard engine. Turbo-Thrift 250 Six not available on Caprice models, Impala Custom Coupe, Sport Sedan or Convertible.

Transmissions

- ☐ 3-Speed fully synchronized (standard with standard engines)
- ☐ Powerglide automatic
- ☐ Turbo Hydra-matic

New options for '70

- ☐ Headlight delay system
- ☐ Finger-tip windshield wiper control
- ☐ Electric power trunk opener
- ☐ Electric power door lock system
- ☐ Automatic seat back lock release

Popular extras

- ☐ Variable-ratio power steering
- ☐ Power disc brakes (standard on Caprice Coupe, Caprice Sedan and Impala Custom Coupe)
- ☐ AM, AM/FM or AM/FM/Stereo radio
- ☐ Stereo tape system with AM or AM/FM/Stereo radio
- ☐ Vinyl roof cover (black, white, dark blue, dark gold, dark green)
- ☐ Electro-Clear rear-window defroster
- ☐ Air conditioning
- ☐ Wheel covers (in several styles)

All illustrations and specifications contained in this literature are based on the latest product information available at the time of publication approval. The right is reserved to make changes at any time without notice in prices, colors, materials, equipment, specifications and models, and to discontinue models. Chevrolet Motor Division, General Motors Corporation, Detroit, Michigan 48202.

Putting you first, keeps us first. **CHEVROLET**

SOURCE BOOKS!

1. GTO (Bonsall)
2. Firebird, 1967-1981 (Bonsall)
3. AMX (Campbell)
4. Chrysler 300 (Bonsall)
5. Chevelle SS (Lehwald)
6. 4-4-2 (Casteele)
7. Charger (Shields)
8. Javelin (Campbell)
9. Corvette, 1953-1967 (Steffen)
10. Nova SS (Lehwald)
11. Barracuda/Challenger (Shields)
12. Road Runner (Shields)
13. Corvette, 1968-1982 (Steffen)
14. Cougar, 1967-1976 (Bonsall)
15. Trans Am, 1967-1981 (Bonsall)
16. El Camino (Lehwald)
17. Big Chevys, 1955-1970 (Lehwald)
18. Big Pontiacs, 1955-1970 (Bonsall)*
*February, 1984

All Volumes $12.95 each plus $2.25 handling.